Creative QUILTING

FOREWORD

The charm of an old patchwork quilt can't be explained by the sum of its parts. Whether it is a simple pattern of large squares sewn and tied, or a masterpiece of tiny pieces with beautiful quilting, the quilt has a special appeal because it is a unique piece of work, at once decorative and useful, and often made with the heart as well as the hands. In a materialistic world, it also has the appeal of something that money can't buy.

The earliest patchwork quilts were made by frugal, rural women who stitched utilitarian bed covers from saved pieces of worn-out garments, or scraps from other projects. Later, mill workers in Britain, North America and Australia used samples from woollen mills. Sometimes these quilts were roughly sewn, but usually with an eye to the pleasing effect produced by placing one colour or tone against another.

Ladies of greater means saved precious pieces of special fabrics – chintzes, silks and satins, to make beautiful appliqué, pieced and crazy patchwork quilts.

The mosaic type of patchwork is probably the earliest style, developing an all-over effect from simple templates, such as hexagons, which were often pieced over papers. The medallion style, which was built up around the central square, was common in England. Now in the Australian National Gallery, the quilt made by convict women on the ship Rajah, is a good example.

In America, the method of sewing together identical blocks was highly developed into a folk art. The early pieced patterns, such as Log Cabin and Star of Bethlehem, which crossed the Atlantic with early settlers, were adapted and new designs flourished. The revival of interest in quiltmaking, especially since the United States Bicentenary, has been remarkable and reflects a new appreciation of traditional skills.

The making of a quilt needs only simple sewing skills – a running stitch for hand-piecing and hand-quilting, slipstitch for binding and a straight machine stitch for piecing blocks and sewing on bindings. It is a help to have a good eye for straight lines, or at least some respect for the grain of the fabric.

CONTENTS

The art in quiltmaking lies in choosing a design and fabrics that are complementary and pleasing. Spend the time to consider these elements before starting. There is something very satisfying in completing a quilt, not the least of which is that it will last. A simple design of squares, machine-pieced and tied, is quick to make and will add visual delight to a room. A simply pieced design, with lots of fine hand-quilting, may take a long time to make, but it will have an heirloom quality that a mass-produced bedcover can never imitate. An added bonus to the quilter is the time it allows to contemplate while quilting – a wonderful luxury in a busy world.

Margot Child

Above: Add a burst of colour to your home with the Chicken Wall Quilt (p. 76)
Far left: The charm of a pile of traditional pieced quilts
Left: Cutting fabric with a rotary (Olfa) cutter for the Log Cabin quilt (p. 20)

Craft Editor: Tonia Todman
Managing Editor: Judy Poulos
Editorial Consultant: Beryl Hodges
Editorial Coordinator: Margaret Kelly
Production Manager: Sheridan Carter
Layout: Lulu Dougherty
Finished Art: Stephen Joseph
Cover Design: Christie & Eckermann
Illustrations: Lesley Griffith
Photography: Harm Mol, Andrew Elton
Publisher: Philippa Sandall

Printed by Toppan Printing Co, Hong Kong

Distributed by J.B. Fairfax Press Pty Ltd
9 Trinity Centre, Park Farm Estate
Wellingborough, Northants
Ph: (0933) 402330 Fax: (0933) 402234

ISBN 1 86343 073 3 (pbk)
ISBN 1 85391 258 1

Formatted by J.B. Fairfax Press Pty Ltd
Output by Adtype, Sydney

The Quilt Story

Quilting is both an art, rich in creativity, and a craft with all the pleasures of working on a project with skill and quiet enjoyment.

THE QUILTER'S CUPBOARD

Just like any other craft, successful quilting depends on having the right equipment to do the job. If you are already a sewer, you are more than likely to have some of the things you need at home already – such as a tape measure, needles, scissors and so on. There are, however, a few pieces you will need to buy and it's a good idea to buy the best that you can afford when it comes to equipment you will want to use again and again. There is nothing more frustrating than trying to cut along a straight line with a pair of blunt scissors. You'll chew up so much fabric that it would have been cheaper to buy good scissors in the beginning.

This is a list of the equipment you are likely to need, although you may not need everything on the list for every quilt.

SCISSORS

A good pair of scissors is essential and ideally you should have three pairs, including a large pair of dressmaker's shears, a smaller pair for delicate cutting and the fiddly bits, and a third pair for cutting paper and templates. It is a good idea to reserve your good dressmaker's shears for cutting fabric, to keep them in the best condition.

PINS

Glass-headed pins are ideal for patchwork and quilting. You may like to use pins of different lengths for different purposes. Longer pins are handy for pinning through a number of layers of fabric and batting. Even better than ordinary pins for this purpose, are medium-sized safety pins which hold the work together quite securely and are a speedier solution than basting with a needle and thread. We call this pin-basting.

NEEDLES

For hand-piecing, use a fine needle you are comfortable with. Sharps are suitable for the purpose. For hand-quilting, you will need size 8 or 9 Betweens. As these are quite short there will be times when you may need a longer needle as well and Sharps are again suitable.

For machine-piecing and machine-quilting, you will need a machine needle suitable for the thickness of your fabrics. Be ruthless – throw away needles as soon as they lose their sharpness. In fact, it is a good idea to begin each project with a new needle.

CUTTER

The rotary or Olfa cutter is a great boon to the quilter. A great labour saver, it allows you to cut several layers of fabric at one time without distortion. You should use a rotary cutter in conjunction with a good plastic ruler and a self-healing mat, made especially for the purpose.

RULERS

Avoid wooden rulers and choose one made from plastic or metal instead. The plastic ones have the dual advantages of being quite sturdy and allowing you to see through the ruler to the fabric or paper beneath. Craft shops sell excellent plastic rulers especially made for quilting that have several marked reference points to assist you to cut straight and accurately. The drawback with these rulers is that they are marked in imperial measurements, so you will need to convert all your measurements. There is a comprehensive Metric/Imperial Conversion chart on page 15.

SEWING MACHINE

Consider your sewing machine as an extension of yourself while stitching a quilt! Your machine needs to be clean and oiled at all times to keep it running properly, and your machine needle needs replacing frequently. Bernina machines with a knee-lift lever for the presser foot are a positive gift to quilters, as they allow you to keep two hands on your work at all times.

THIMBLES

Smooth quilting technique always demands that you use at least one thimble and perhaps two – a metal one for the third finger of the upper hand and a leather one for the finger underneath to protect it.

THREAD

Good quality machine thread should be used for hand or machine-piecing. For hand-quilting, it is best to use cotton quilting thread. It is stronger than the usual machine thread and comes in a good variety of colours. In the past, threads have been treated by passing them through beeswax (some books still recommend it) but it is no longer necessary with the excellent quilting threads available today.

The colour of the thread for piecing should blend with the fabrics so you can work with only one colour and not have to keep re-threading the needle. You can buy nylon monofilament thread at good quilting shops. This has the advantage of being 'invisible' and therefore suitable for all colours. It should be used as the top thread only, with an ordinary machine sewing thread in the bobbin.

PENCILS

A soft, sharp lead pencil for tracing around templates is essential. These days you can buy water-soluble pencils and pens, especially made for quilters, including a silver pencil that will mark both light and dark fabrics. Make sure that whatever you choose will either fade out or wash out without leaving a permanent mark.

TEMPLATES

A template is a precisely drawn and cut shape for a pattern piece. Some templates for hand-piecing, such as the shell, hexagon and diamond, are available from craft shops but it is not difficult to make your own. If the template is not going to be used too often, then cardboard (perhaps strengthened with tape) is quite suitable. Sandpaper is also useful as it tends to grip the fabric as you work. The problem with both of these options is that they are very subject to wear and tear, especially around the edges. If you do use cardboard, it is a good idea to cut a number of templates rather than relying on just one. If the template is going to be used many times or if the particular project is a big one, then you would be wise to cut your template out of firm plastic or acetate, available from quilting and art supply shops. Whichever material you choose, you will need the usual drawing aids (set square, protractor, pencil, ruler etc) as well as a sharp craft knife or scissors for cutting out the template. Draw your shape carefully onto the template material, using a ruler to achieve straight lines. Carefully cut out the shape with a sharp craft knife or scissors. In this book, templates for tracing are supplied.

Supplied by Natalie Wise

HOOPS AND FRAMES

Quilting hoops are essential on all but the smallest hand-quilted projects to achieve a smooth finish. A quilting hoop consists of two wooden rings, one of which fits closely inside the other. The fabric is stretched over the inner ring and then secured with the outer ring. Take care not to stretch the fabric too tightly. A hoop of about 40 cm is a good size to work with. You can also buy a quilting hoop on a stand or, if the project is a large one, use a free-standing quilting frame if you find one comfortable to work with. You can also buy small hoops, specially made for machine-quilting.

MATERIAL MATTERS

You can always tell a true quilter by the bulging bags and drawers full of fascinating scraps of fabric, squirrelled away for future use. And actually, this is one of the most delightful aspects of quilting – that even when you're not actually working on a project, you can be planning and designing, waiting for the coincidence of two scraps of fabric to trigger your imagination.

CHOOSING YOUR FABRIC

A quilt is basically a sandwich with a filling, the batting or wadding, between two layers of fabric. The filling is held in place by the stitches of the quilting or by the tying. Any fabric which keeps its shape when stretched with two hands along the grain can be used for quilting.

The choice of fabrics and colours is crucial to the success of a quilt. You can use patterns and plains of just about every kind, but some fabrics are obviously better suited than others. Smooth, closely woven, dress-weight cottons are ideal for quilting. Linen, lightweight wool, silk or sateen also work well. Avoid synthetic or stretchy fabrics as they are more difficult to manage. Velvet gives a lovely texture to patchwork, but you will need a little more experience to manage its foibles. Whichever you choose, make sure all your fabrics are of the same, or very similar, weight.

Some quite heavy fabrics, like tweed or wool, can look very effective, but are a great challenge for the hand-quilter. It is best to reserve these for machine-quilting. At the other end of the scale, very sheer fabrics can also give you quilters' nightmares! If you must use one because it is just right and there is no substitute, line it first with a dress-weight cotton.

Small prints, florals and checks are ideal for quilting, but bolder prints can also be effective. To get an impression of how the finished quilt will look, drape the fabrics over a chair in roughly the proportions you will be using them and then stand back and consider. You will be able to tell how well the colours and patterns work together or whether you need to make changes. Stripes can be very effective, but take care – they will show any faults if your cutting and sewing are not perfectly straight. The difference between a mediocre quilt and an outstanding one is often because of the way the quilter has used light, shade and colour to complement the patchwork. Experiment with combinations of colour and pattern – you will learn with experience which combinations work best.

BACKING

Choose a pure cotton fabric for the quilt back, washing and preparing it in the same way as the fabrics for the quilt top. For a large quilt, you may have to join fabrics to achieve the width of backing required. If you are new to quilting, choose a print fabric for the backing rather than a plain one – it is much more forgiving of the odd uneven stitch.

PREPARING YOUR FABRIC

It is crucial to wash (preferably in a washing machine) cotton fabrics before you cut. Washing will pre-shrink the fabric and take out the excess dye and any chemical sizing. The dye in some fabrics can run and stain the others, so wash any likely culprits by hand to test for colour fastness. Iron the fabrics while they are still damp. Remove all the selvages before you begin cutting.

BATTING

Batting, or wadding as it is also known, is the filling in the 'quilt sandwich'. In days past, any thick material, such as flannel or even an old quilt, was used for batting. These days the most commonly used batting is made from polyester fibre. It is available in a variety of widths and thicknesses and has the advantage of being lightweight, washable and non-allergenic. Traditional cotton batting is still used but is much heavier than the polyester version and the finished quilt will have to be dry cleaned. Take care with cotton batting because it tends to move around and bunch up in spots. Close quilting will help to prevent this happening. Batting which is not too hard to the touch is the easiest to sew. It should be bonded to prevent fibres migrating through the quilt.

Wool batting gives a wonderful warmth and softness to a quilt. Cotton/polyester batting is also available. Like your quilting fabrics, it has to be pre-washed as the cotton content shrinks. For hand-quilting, it is better to choose the thinner batting, which gives the traditional look, and keep the thicker types for machine-quilted and tied quilts, which sometimes look more like comforters.

QUILTING SKILLS

Quilting is not difficult. If you can sew a simple running stitch, you can make a quilt. There are a few simple principles and techniques which will help you.

MARKING FABRIC

Always mark the fabric on the wrong side with a sharp pencil, dark for light fabric and light or silver for dark fabric. Test the marker for washability on a scrap of fabric first. Place the template on the fabric with a straight edge following the grainline. Some templates will even have the grainline marked for you.

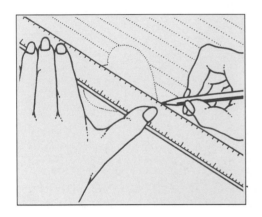

Left: Use a plastic ruler and sharp pencil to mark lines and templates on your fabric

CUTTING OUT

Pieced quilting requires the cutting of dozens of small shapes. The quickest way to cut a quantity of the same piece is to cut three or four thicknesses of fabric together. Using a rotary cutter and cutting mat is the easiest way to cut strips. Otherwise you will need to

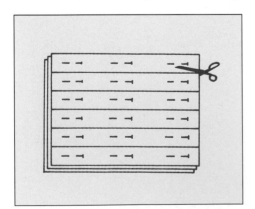

Left: Cutting out a large number of strips using the multi-layered method

pin the fabric layers together, placing the pins inside the cutting line which is marked on the top layer. Cut out the shape carefully with good, sharp scissors,

taking particular care with the corners. This method is suitable only if you can work without marked seamlines. For all hand-piecing and some machine-piecing, pencilled seamlines are essential. Trace around the template with a sharp pencil then cut out with a seam allowance added, usually 6 mm. The pencil lines you have drawn become your sewing line.

SEWING

There are two easy quilting principles you should follow:

1 Sew in straight lines and avoid sewing into corners if possible.

2 Join small pieces together to form larger ones and then join those into even larger ones and continue in this way. Often you will sew several steps to make the basic block of the quilt and then join the blocks together to complete the quilt top.

Pieces are always joined with right sides facing, except for appliqué.

MACHINE-PIECING OR HAND-PIECING

Machine-piecing is the quickest way of joining patchwork but there are occasions when handsewing is preferable, such as when you need to sew in angles or carefully match difficult points. Equally, some quilts are best machine-pieced, such as the *Log Cabin* and *Seminole* designs. In truth, quilters who choose hand-piecing do so, not for practical reasons, but for the pleasure of relaxing hand work and its portability.

Before you begin sewing, you will need to establish a reference for the seam allowance. If the distance from the needle to the edge of the presser

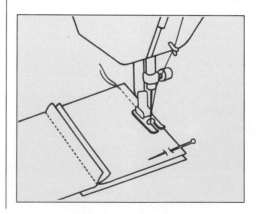

Left: Machine-piecing patches together into a strip

foot is 6 mm, then you can place the edge of the presser foot on the edge of the fabric to achieve the exact seam allowance. If this is not the case on your machine, you can use any lines marked on the foot plate or mark your own with masking tape.

Pin the pieces together with right sides facing, placing the pins at right angles to the seamline. There is no need to backstitch at this stage because seams will be crossed over by others. Sew the patches together along the seamline, sewing right up to the

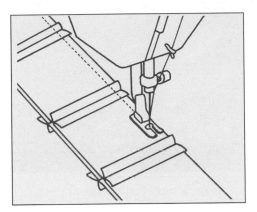

Left: Piecing strips together, sewing across the seams

pins. When you have joined patches into a square or strip, you will need to join that square or strip to others and this will involve sewing across seamlines. Pin and sew as before, taking care to match seamlines and points.

To save time, sew all the same steps for the whole quilt at once, feeding them under the presser foot in a continuous seam. Later, you can cut them apart before joining them in a new combination by the

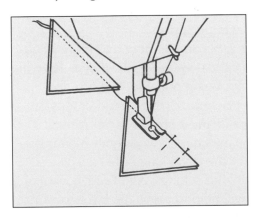

Left: Chainsewing triangles to form pieced squares

same method – chainsewing.

Hand-piecing is the traditional method of joining patchwork both with and without papers. The quilts in this book are all made without papers. Pin the patches together with right sides facing, placing the pins at right angles to the seamline. Sew with small even running stitches, using a size 8 or 9 Sharp needle and quilting cotton (or cotton-covered polyester) thread. Take care not to have your thread too long – about 40 cm is enough. Begin and end the seam with a few backstitches to secure it. When joining patches, take care to match the pencil lines (seamlines) on both sides, sew only between seamlines and do not stitch in the seam allowances.

PRESSING

Always press seams as you work to keep the pieces flat and the seams as sharp as possible. If you are working with very thick fabric, press the seams open. Generally, however, seams pressed to one side are stronger than those pressed open. Press the seam allowances towards the darker fabric to prevent them showing through the lighter one. Take care not to stretch pieces out of shape when pressing.

CONSTRUCTION

Cut the batting and backing a little larger than the finished size required as the quilting itself draws the fabrics in. You can join lengths of backing fabric to achieve the width you require, after removing all the selvages. Press the seam allowances to one side. The backing can be the same size as the quilt top and then all the edges bound together with a separate binding, or you can have the backing fabric fold onto the quilt front to make a self-binding.

To assemble your quilt, lay the backing fabric face down on a table. Place the batting over the top and then the quilt top on top of that, face up. Smooth out any wrinkles and pin the layers together using medium-sized safety pins or baste for hand-quilting if you prefer.

If you are basting, begin at the centre of the quilt and sew towards each corner. Then sew in rows about 10 cm apart over the whole quilt.

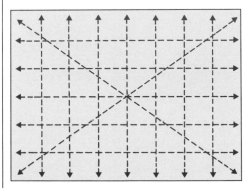

Left: The basting pattern for securing the layers of the quilt

BORDERS

Not all quilts have borders. Some patterns are traditionally made without one, but a border can be used to embellish as well as enlarge a quilt. You can have more than one border. Before you attach the borders, press the quilt top well. Remember that the border should look like an integral part of the design, not an afterthought. Choose a fabric that complements the others in the quilt. To work out the length of your side border strips, measure the quilt top lengthways through the centre – not along the edges. Cut two borders of the desired width to this length. After attaching the side borders, measure the total width of the quilt top, including the side borders, and cut the top and bottom borders to this length. If you wish to mitre the border corners, cut the strips extra long, centre them on each edge of the quilt, sew them on, then join them with a seam at an angle of 45-degrees at each corner.

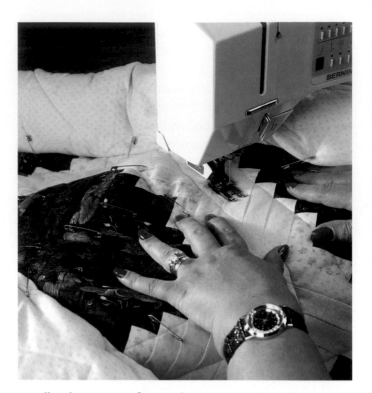

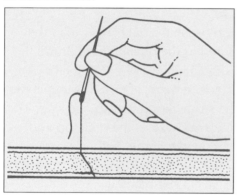

Left: Secure the knotted end of your thread by pulling it into the batting

QUILTING

Quilting by hand should be done using a quilting hoop to keep the layers secure while you work. Use quilting thread colour-matched to the fabric unless you want the stitching to show for a special effect. Thread a size 7 or 8 Between sewing needle with about 40 cm of thread and tie a knot in the end. Begin stitching in the centre of the quilt, inserting the

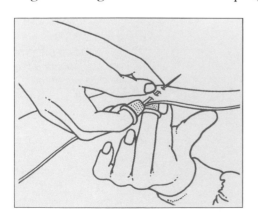

Left: Hand-quilting requires two thimbles for a smooth technique

needle about 2 cm from where you wish to begin. Pull gently on the thread so the knot slips into the batting. Work in small, even running stitches, sewing around the seamlines, outline quilting 6 mm inside the edges of the patches or in patterns that you have drawn onto the fabric. Use a stencil to keep your patterns uniform over the whole of the quilt. When you have finished quilting, end as you began by knotting the thread and running it about 2 cm into the batting before cutting it off, even with the fabric. To move from one motif to another, take the needle under the top layer of your quilt rather than cutting the thread and beginning again.

Machine-quilting is becoming more and more popular. While results appear very quickly, it does have the disadvantage of not being portable. Use a cotton-coated polyester machine sewing thread or a nylon monofilament thread and a size 70 to 90 needle, depending on the thickness of your quilt. You may also need to adjust the stitch length. Do a little test piece to check all your settings. An even-feed walking foot attachment will help to move the layers of your quilt smoothly without effort or bunching. As with hand-quilting, you should begin in the centre of your quilt and work towards the edges. To do this, roll the opposite sides up quite tightly on either side of the presser foot leaving the area to be quilted lying flat in the middle. You can then unroll parts as you need them.

BINDING

When all the quilting is complete, trim back the batting and backing to be even with the quilt top (unless you are going to fold the backing over onto the front to make self binding). Cut your binding

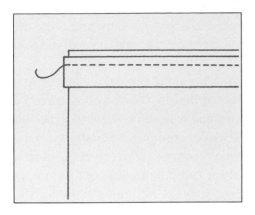

Left: Applying the binding to the top edge of the quilt

strips to the width suggested and the length required for the top, bottom and sides of the quilt, measured through the centre. Fold the strips over double with wrong sides together. Press. Stitch the binding to the sides of the quilt, through all thicknesses, with

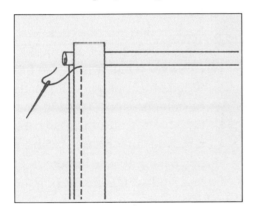

Left: Applying the binding to the side of the quilt, over the top of the previously joined top binding

right sides together and raw edges even. Fold the binding over to the back of the quilt and handsew it into position. Repeat for the top and bottom edges.

MITRING A CORNER

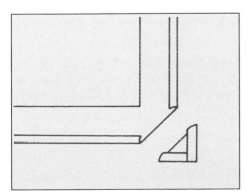

Left: Fold in the raw edge and cut off the corner

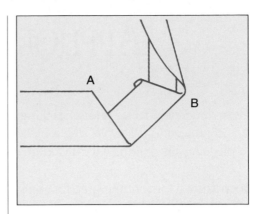

Left: fold in the corner

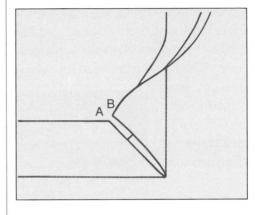

Left: Fold in half the side edges, then fold in the other half so that A meets B

TUFTING OR TYING QUILTS

Some large quilts are not quilted at all in the traditional sense, but are tied. This is particularly useful for quilts where a very thick batting has been used. Using heavy crochet cotton, take a stitch through all the

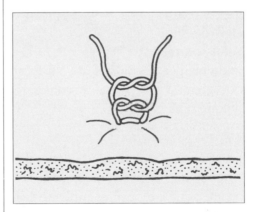

Left: Using thick cotton to tie a quilt

layers of the quilt. Tie the ends together securely twice, but don't pull too tightly. Trim the ends. For very dramatic tufts, use several strands of thread or very thick thread. You can tie a quilt using matching or contrasting cotton. Tie in the seamline or in the centre of the patch, depending on whether you are making a feature of the tying or not. You can tie your quilt on the top, or on the back if you do not wish the tufts to show.

Applique Quilts

Appliqué adds a new dimension to traditional quilting. It can add texture and pattern to a simple single-piece quilt or embellish a pieced quilt, making it a truly unique object.

Appliqué has been known for centuries and for much of that time it has been part of the quilter's art. The advent of inexpensive printed cotton fabrics gave an almost limitless range to the possibilities. One area in which this development was most obvious was in the flourishing of Broderie Perse quilts. This is a technique in which suitable motifs are cut from printed chintz fabric and appliquéd onto a background fabric which can itself be pieced and decorated with stencils and appliqué.

The delight of appliqué is that you can use any pattern or design that takes your fancy. There are many traditional designs that are often seen in appliqué quilts, but be adventurous – design your own. A motif from wallpaper, a picture from a book, a design in a shop window are all useful sources. The photocopier and enlarger at work or at your local library will be your greatest ally when it comes to designing your appliqué quilt.

HAND-APPLIQUE

There are a number of methods of hand-appliqué, the most common ones involving the use of paper patterns. It is important if you are using a repeating appliqué that the shape and size of the piece does not vary too much – that is, of course, unless you want it to. To ensure this uniformity, the quilter makes a paper pattern of the appliqué shape, traces the shape onto the wrong side of the fabric (tracing many of them at a time and adding seam allowances if they are not already included) and cuts them out. If you do not have access to a light box to do your tracing, taping the fabric to a sunlit window will usually do quite well. Pin a paper pattern, following grainlines, to the back of each traced pattern and cut out with a 6 mm seam allowance. Baste the pattern to the fabric, removing the pins as you go. Turn and baste the seam allowance to the wrong side with a small running stitch. Press.

When placing your appliqué pieces, remember that those which are overlapped by others will need to be attached first using a small whipstitch. When the piece is amost completely sewn on, remove the basting and the paper pattern before you complete the stitching. A pair of tweezers is ideal for carefully pulling out the paper pattern without disturbing the stitching. When all the appliqué pieces have been attached, press the quilt top carefully.

If your appliqué piece is quite large and bulky or if the background fabric is showing through, you can cut out the background from the back, leaving a 6 mm border all around.

Doffy White, who made this wonderful appliqué quilt, made her templates out of pliable plastic so they could easily be removed and re-used without her having to cut hundreds of small paper pieces. She repeated the charming appliqué design in the hand-quilting.

MACHINE-APPLIQUE

Appliqué with a sewing machine is quick and easy. It is crucial to know your sewing machine and all its foibles and to keep it in top working order. Always use sharp needles and keep the machine well oiled. If you have a special walking foot that feeds the fabric evenly through the machine you will find your work even easier. You can also buy a quilting guide for accurate stitching.

You can machine-appliqué using a paper pattern as for hand-appliqué or you can use the Broderie Perse method. In either case, a small zigzag stitch is ideal for stitching the motifs to your quilt. Iron-on interfacing or bonding web is used by some quilters to attach their motifs before stitching. Experiment to find the method that best suits you and your quilt.

Metric/Imperial Conversion Chart

All the measurements in this book are given in metric. If you prefer to work in imperial measurements, or if your equipment is marked in imperial measurements, use this chart to convert from one to the other. The conversions can only be the closest approximation, so it is crucial that you work only in imperial OR metric – not both. It does not matter which one you choose as long as you stay with your choice all the way through.

6 mm	$^1/_4$ in	25 cm	10 in
1 cm	$^1/_2$ in	30 cm	12 in
12 mm	$^1/_2$ in	35 cm	14 in
1.5 cm	$^3/_4$ in	40 cm	16 in
2 cm	$^3/_4$ in	45 cm	18 in
3 cm	$1^1/_4$ in	50 cm	20 in
4 cm	$1^1/_2$ in	60 cm	24 in
5 cm	2 in	70 cm	28 in
6 cm	$2^1/_2$ in	80 cm	32 in
7 cm	3 in	90 cm	36 in
8 cm	$3^1/_4$ in	1 m	40 in
9 cm	$3^1/_2$ in	115 cm	45 in
10 cm	4 in	150 cm	60 in
12 cm	$4^3/_4$ in	2 m	$2^1/_4$ yds
13 cm	$5^1/_4$ in	2.5 m	$2^3/_4$ yds
15 cm	6 in	3 m	$3^1/_4$ yds
17 cm	7 in	4 m	$4^1/_2$ yds
20 cm	8 in	5 m	$5^1/_2$ yds

Traditional Quilts

For centuries, piecing fabrics together into quilts of intricate design has been a much-loved craft. Few examples of the earliest patchwork quilts remain, but the more recent history is richly illustrated with beautiful pieces such as these.

LOG CABIN QUILTS

Log Cabin quilts are among the most popular traditional quilt patterns. Follow Kate McEwen's step-by-step guide to making your own Log Cabin quilt on the following pages.

Log Cabin quilts are ideal for beginners and the pattern can be easily adapted to smaller projects such as cushions, pot holders and placemats. Our step-by-step quilt is a *Log Cabin* quilt in the *Barn Raising* style, one of the most popular quilt patterns. It can be a true scrapbag quilt, utilising quite small pieces of fabric where the only governing factor is the contrast between light and dark colours.

Like all *Log Cabin* quilts, it is based on the pattern of light and dark rectangles, pieced around a centre square. The rectangles are laid in such a way as to represent the logs used by the early American settlers to build their cabins. Some early quilts even

had a little chimney sewn in to further underline the theme. The centre square of the block is often red, to denote the fireplace, or yellow, to represent the lighted window.

These days, most *Log Cabin* quilts are made from light and dark printed, dress-weight cottons but, in the past, quilters often used wool as well. Mixing silks, velvets, and other 'luxury' fabrics produces a lovely quilt with quite a different feeling about it. Traditional *Log Cabin* quilts were made without a border, but this is not a hard-and-fast rule and these days quilters often add a plain or print border.

While the basic ingredients of a *Log Cabin* block remain the same – half in light and half in dark rectangles, changing the way in which the rectangles are placed or the blocks are joined will give you quite a different looking quilt. Joining the blocks so that the dark halves are adjacent to one another and the light halves are adjacent to one another, gives a design of alternating light and dark diamonds. Piecing the blocks and joining them so that the dark and light halves form alternating diagonals, reminiscent of a roof line, makes this design known as *Barn Raising*. Placing the blocks so that the dark and light halves travel diagonally across the quilt creates the pattern known as *Straight Furrow*. Making a block so that the light and dark quarters are opposite their mates, and joining the blocks side by side across the row, makes yet another pattern called *Courthouse Steps*.

Left: Make this Log Cabin quilt following the instructions on pages 20-23

Left: A charming Log Cabin quilt combining subtle colours and prints for a real country look

Below left: This charming placemat is simply one Log Cabin block with a stencilled design painted into the centre square. To complete the placemat, assemble the top, batting, backing and binding as for a quilt

Below: Log Cabin quilts depend on the arrangement of light and dark fabrics for their effect

19

CREATE A QUILT

FINISHED SIZE

Quilt: 180 cm x 225 cm
(approximately)
Block size: 22.5 cm (approximately)
Total number of full blocks: 48

FABRIC QUANTITIES

20 cm of colour 1 (red)
20 cm of colour 2 (dark)
30 cm of colour 3 (light)
40 cm of colour 4 (dark)
45 cm of colour 5 (light)
55 cm of colour 6 (dark)
1.5 m of colour 7 (light), this includes
    fabric for the first border
1.2 m of colour 8 (dark), this includes
    fabric for the second border
185 cm x 230 cm backing fabric,
    pieced from 4.6 m of 115 cm
    wide fabric
185 cm x 230 cm wadding
    an additional 60 cm of colour 8
    for the binding

NOTIONS

safety pins, pins, needles and scissors
sewing thread
sewing machine
pencil and ruler
rotary (Olfa) cutter and mat

CUTTING

6 mm seam allowances are included in
the cutting instructions.

1 You will need to cut your fabric
into strips by folding the fabric in
half, selvage to selvage, and then
again so you have four layers. If you
are using a rotary (Olfa) cutter you can
put about three lots of fabric, folded
this way, on top of each other and cut
them all at once. An Olfa cutter is
ideal for a *Log Cabin* quilt and means
that seam allowances are already
included in the cutting instructions.
Cut all the fabric into 4 cm strips. You
will need:
2 strips of red, cut into 4 cm squares
5 strips of colour 2
7 strips of colour 3
9 strips of colour 4
11 strips of colour 5
13 strips of colour 6
16 strips of colour 7
19 strips of colour 8

Step 2

CONSTRUCTION

2 Take the pile of red squares and
one strip of colour 2. Lay the strip
under the presser foot of your sewing

Step 1: Using a specially
marked plastic ruler, rotary
cutter and mat to cut multiple
fabric layers
Step 2: Chainsewing all the
red squares to the first dark
strip

Step 1

machine (right side up) and lay the red squares on top one by one (right side down), stitching them together in a 6 mm seam. Sew all the red squares in this way. Finger press the seams to lie flat and cut the strips apart so you have a red square joined to a colour 2 square.

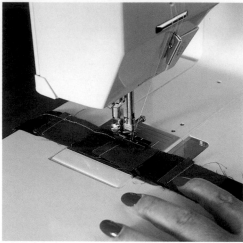

Step 3

3 Take the other strips of colour 2 and lay them down one by one (face up) under your presser foot and sew the previously joined red and colour 2 squares down onto these strips. Always place the segment just sewn at the top when placing the block on the next strip to be sewn. Finger press the seams to lie flat. Cut the newly formed squares apart, even with the edges of the dark and red squares.

Step 4

4 Place the first light strip (colour 3) under the presser foot as you did for the colour 2 strip and join the just completed squares as before. Cut them apart, even with the edges as before. Finger press the seams to lie flat.

5 Add the second strip of colour 3 as before and continue in this way, sewing two strips of the same colour to each square until all the colours have been sewn to the block. Always place at the top the segment just sewn when placing the block on the next strip to be sewn. Finger press the seams to lie flat. Cut the newly formed squares apart, even with the edges of the black and red squares.

Step 5

6 When the forty-eight blocks are complete, arrange them, six blocks across and eight blocks down, as shown for the *Barn Raising* pattern. Sew the blocks together, making sure to match the seams where necessary. Press the quilt top carefully.

7 Attach a border to your quilt if you feel it needs one. Borders can be used to extend a quilt to whatever size you need. We have used two borders – one out of light fabric 8.8 cm wide and the other out of dark fabric 13.8 cm wide. To make the light border, measure the length of your

Step 3: Joining the piece made in Step 2 to another dark strip
Step 4: Using exactly the same procedure as in Step 3, join in the first light strip
Step 5: The completed block for the quilt, with the red square slightly off centre. Note that there are two more dark strips than there are light strips in the block

quilt top through the centre. Cut two strips of fabric this length and 10 cm wide. Join fabric if necessary to make the required length. Sew these to the side edges of the quilt top in 6 mm seams. Measure the total width of the quilt top, including the borders you have just joined on, again measuring through the centre. Cut two strips of fabric this length, joining strips if necessary, and 10 cm wide. Sew these to the top and bottom edges of the quilt in 6 mm seams. Make the dark border in exactly the same way, cutting the strips 15 cm wide.

QUILTING

8 Place backing fabric on a table, right side down and sticky tape it down to stop it from slipping. Place the batting on top and then the pieced quilt on top of that, facing upwards. Pin through all three layers with safety pins to hold the quilt together while you are machine or hand-quilting. *Log Cabin* quilts can also be tied in the traditional way. We have quilted this quilt by machine, stitching diagonally through the centre of each block, changing the direction of the diagonal for each quarter of the quilt. Take the stitching through the light border as well. Make another row of stitches in between each pair of rows just made.

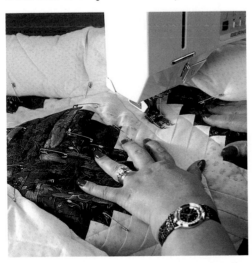

Step 8

Above: Detail of the diagonal machine-quilting
Step 8: Quilting by machine, showing the quilted parts rolled up out of the way

The dark border has been quilted with rows of parallel stitching about 5 cm apart. Trim away any excess batting and backing.

FINISHING

9 To bind the edges of the quilt, cut four 8 cm wide strips for the top, bottom and sides. Measure through the centre of the quilt as before to determine the length of the strips. Join strips if necessary to achieve the required length. Press the strips over double with wrong sides together. Sew the binding to the right side of both sides of the quilt with raw edges even. Fold the binding over to the wrong side of the quilt and handsew into place. Repeat the measuring and sewing steps described in Step 7 for the top and bottom binding.

SINGLE IRISH CHAIN

Margot Child designed and made this beautiful quilt which is simplicity itself. Made from only two fabrics, a creamy white and contrasting crisp blue cotton, it relies for its charm on the delicate stitching of the hand-quilting.

FABRIC SUGGESTIONS

The blocks in this quilt are set at an angle, travelling diagonally across the quilt. For a slightly different look, make this quilt in two tones of the same colour.

The quilt has been machine-pieced and hand-quilted.

FINISHED SIZE

Quilt: 215 cm x 190 cm (approximately)
Block size: 15 cm x 15 cm
Total number of blocks: 162
Total number of border triangles: 34
Total number of half triangles: 4

FABRIC QUANTITIES

4 m of 115 cm wide white fabric
2 m of 115 cm wide blue fabric
200 cm x 225 cm backing fabric, pieced from 4 m of 115 cm wide fabric
222 cm x 200 cm batting

NOTIONS

cardboard or template plastic
pencil and ruler
rotary (Olfa) cutter and mat
safety pins, pins, needles and scissors
sewing thread and quilting thread
sewing machine

CUTTING

Do not forget to add seam allowances to each piece you cut.

1 Cut ninety white fabric squares 15 cm x 15 cm plus seam allowances. Cut thirty-eight blue fabric triangles from template **a**, adding seam allowances on all sides. Cut four blue fabric half-triangles from template **b** for the corners adding seam allowances on all sides. Cut strips of blue and white fabric 5 cm wide plus seam allowances.

With this quilt it is particularly important to match the grainlines on the template and fabric in order not to be left with a bias edge on your quilt.

CONSTRUCTION

See the Pull Out Pattern Sheet at the back of the book for the additional quilting designs.

2 Piece the strips together in threes, one-third with two whites and a blue in the middle and two-thirds with two blues and a white in the middle. Press the seams to the blue side. Cut the joined strips into 5 cm lengths plus seam allowances.

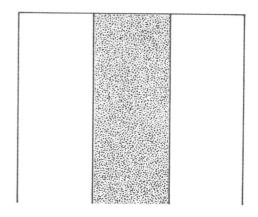

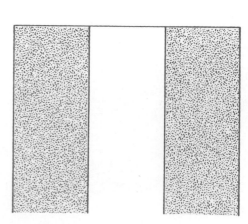

3 Join the strips made in Step 2 in a chequerboard pattern to make seventy-two 9-patch blocks, each with a blue square in the centre. Press.

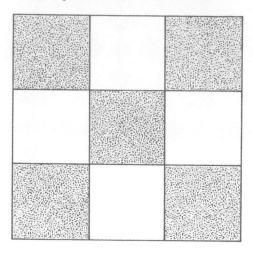

4 Join these blocks to form rows, alternating large white squares with the chequerboard blocks and placing a white square on each end. Press. Note that the number of blocks in a row depends on the position of the row in the quilt. You will need: two single white blocks; two rows of three blocks; two rows of five blocks; two rows of seven blocks; two rows of nine blocks; two rows of eleven blocks; two rows of thirteen blocks; two rows of fifteen blocks and two rows of seventeen blocks.

5 At this point it is a good idea to lay your quilt out as it will look when finished. Pin the short side of a blue triangle to the end of each row, so that the long sides of all the triangles form the straight sides of the quilt. Sew the triangles in place. Press.

6 Join all the rows to form the quilt top, sewing a blue half-triangle to every corner square. Press the quilt top carefully.

QUILTING

7 One quilting design appears on the opposite page, two others are on the pattern sheet. Trace the quilting designs and make stencils/templates of them, using firm plastic. Transfer the designs to the quilt top using the template and a lead pencil.

8 Lay the backing fabric face down on a table. Place the batting on top and then the quilt top, face up, on top of that. Baste or pin-baste all the layers together.

9 Hand-quilt the quilt top, stitching along the pencil lines and approximately 6 mm inside the small squares as shown.

FINISHING

10 Trim the quilt top and batting so that approximately 3 cm of the backing fabric protrudes all around. Turn the backing over onto the quilt top, folding in the corners twice to form a neat mitre (see page 13). Turn under 1 cm on the raw edge and handsew the folded edges and the corners into place.

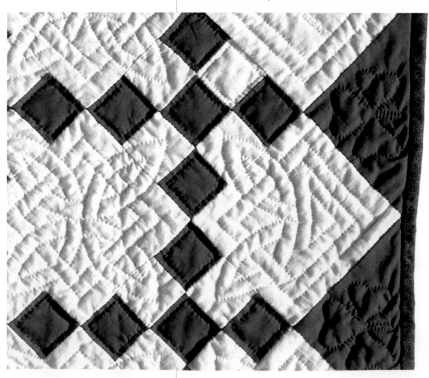

Left: Detail of the Single Irish Chain quilt showing the hand-quilting

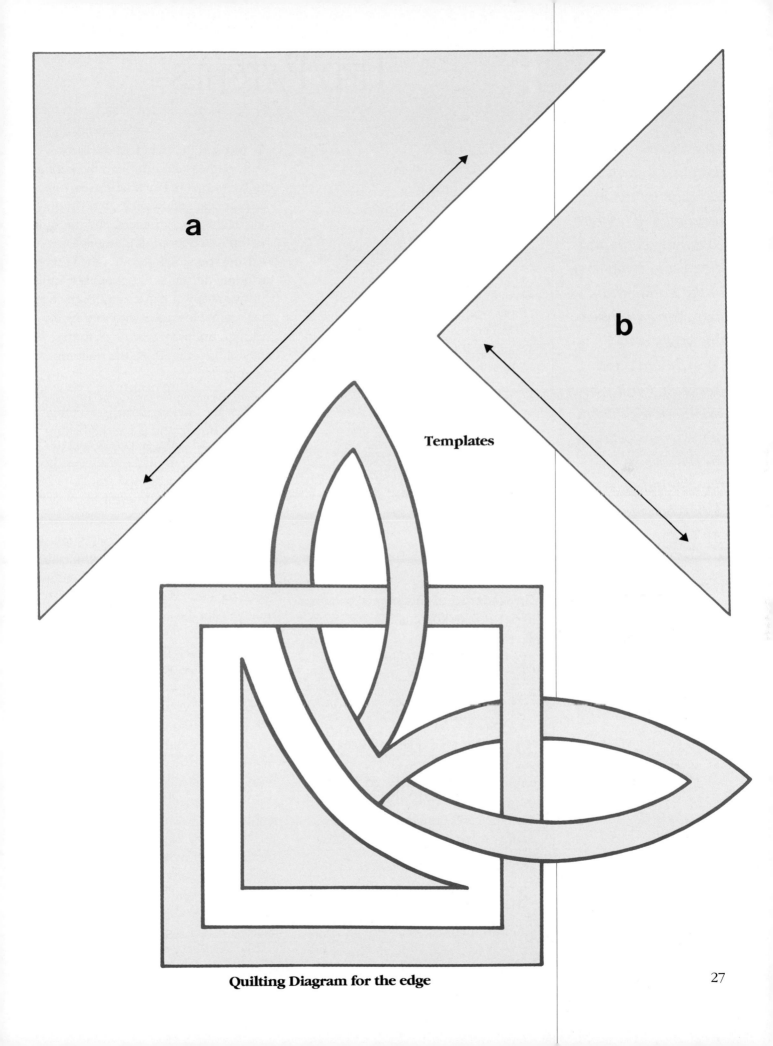

a

b

Templates

Quilting Diagram for the edge

27

TIED PATCHES

Marie Grove designed and made this quilt by piecing rectangles of brightly coloured cotton and then hand-tying them in the traditional way. You can make this bright and cheerful quilt in a weekend. Quilt it by sewing in the ditches of the seams between the patches or hand-quilting a design over the whole quilt top.

FINISHED SIZE

Quilt: 140 cm x 200 cm
(approximately)
Block size: 30 cm x 20 cm

FABRIC QUANTITIES

36 rectangles of cotton fabric, in as
many colours as possible
150 cm x 210 cm (approximately)
backing fabric, pieced from 3 m of
115 cm wide fabric
1.5 m black fabric for the borders and
binding
150 cm x 210 cm (approximately)
batting

NOTIONS

thick crochet cotton for tying
safety pins, pins, needles and scissors
rotary (Olfa) cutter and mat
plastic ruler and pencil
sewing thread
sewing machine

CUTTING

Do not forget to add seam allowances
to each piece you cut.

1 Cut all the rectangles to 30 cm x
20 cm plus seam allowances. A
rotary cutter will save time.

CONSTRUCTION

2 Lay out your quilt top (with six
rectangles across and six down)
and experiment with the arrangement.
Join the top row together and then
the next row. Continue in this way
until you have six rows. Press. Mark
them 1, 2, 3, 4, 5 and 6.

3 Join the six rows to complete the
quilt top, following the order
you have marked. Press.

4 Measure the width of the quilt
top, measuring through the centre.
Cut two strips of black fabric, each 9
cm plus seam allowances wide and as
long as this measurement. Sew these to
the top and bottom of the quilt top.
Measure the length through the centre,
including the top and bottom borders.
Cut two strips of black fabric 9 cm wide
plus seam allowances and as long as
this measurement. Sew these to the
sides of the quilt. Press the quilt top
carefully.

5 Lay the backing fabric on a table,
face down, and place the batting
on top. Place the quilt top on top of
that, face upwards. Baste or pin-baste
through all thicknesses.

TYING

6 Using heavy crochet cotton, take a
stitch at each corner and the centre
of the rectangles. Tie the ends together
twice securely, but don't pull too
tightly. Trim the ends. For a more
dramatic effect, use several strands of
thread. Tie each one at these points.
Trim off any excess backing and batting.

FINISHING

7 Measure the width of the quilt as
before, to find the length of binding required. Cut two strips of black
fabric, each 8 cm wide and as long as
this measurement. Press the strips over
double with wrong sides together. Sew
the binding to the top and bottom of
the quilt with right sides facing and raw
edges even. Turn the binding to the
wrong side and handsew into place.
Repeat this process for binding the side
edges.

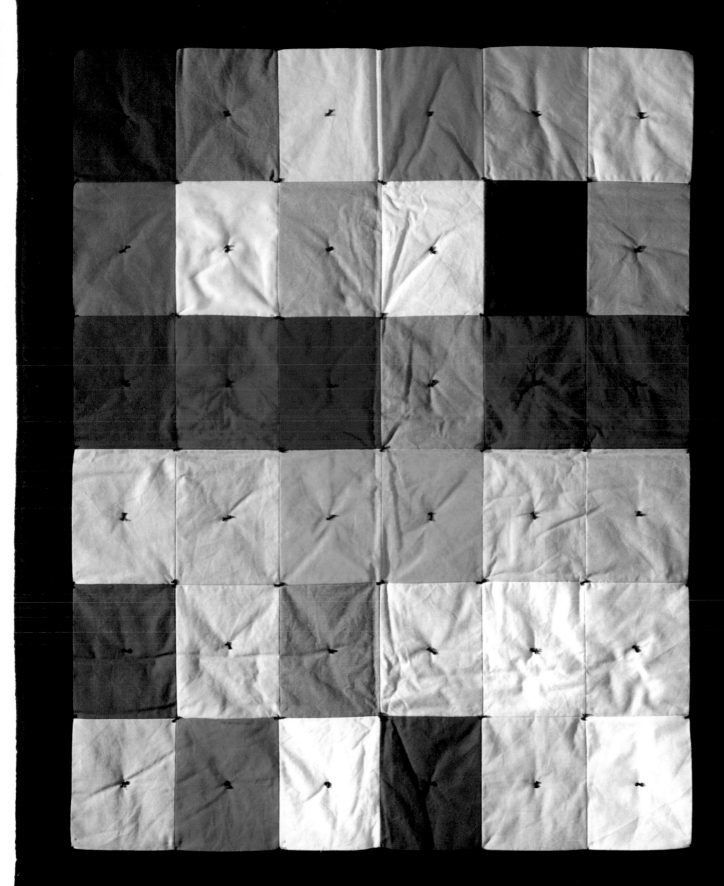

BITS AND PIECES

This delightfully 'homey' quilt was made from an almost countless variety of cotton seersucker prints which were popular for pyjamas in the 1950s and 1960s. Dorothy Mitchell was lucky enough to acquire them, brand new, in the form of a sample book which had somehow been put away and forgotten.

FABRIC SUGGESTIONS

The same design would lend itself just as well to any small prints, gingham or checks but not to a large print fabric. It is an ideal project for strip cutting, using a rotary cutter. 6 mm seam allowances have been included.

FINISHED SIZE

Quilt: 175 cm x 213 cm (approximately)
Block size: 34 cm (approximately)
Total number of full blocks: 12

FABRIC QUANTITIES

a wide variety of cotton print fabrics
2 m of plain cotton fabric for the borders
185 cm x 225 cm cotton fabric for the backing (pieced from 3.7 m of 115 cm wide fabric)
185 cm x 225 cm batting

NOTIONS

rotary (Olfa) cutter and mat
plastic ruler
safety pins, pins, needles and scissors
sewing thread
sewing machine

CUTTING

1 Cut 5 cm wide strips across the width of the cotton print fabrics.

CONSTRUCTION

2 Join three 5 cm wide strips together to form a strip 12.6 cm wide. Press.

3 Cut this strip along its length into 12.6 cm squares.

4 Repeat steps 1 and 2, varying the fabric combinations, until you have 108 squares.

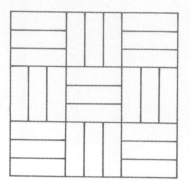

5 To form the block, join nine of these squares into rows of three, alternating horizontal and vertical strips, making a block 35.4 cm square.

6 Join several 5 cm wide strips at their short ends to form a long strip. From this long strip, cut 8 sashes each 35.4 cm long. Do not worry too much about where the joins fall – it is interesting to have them fall in an irregular way.

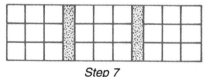

Step 7

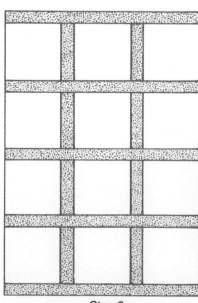

Step 8

7 Join three blocks horizontally with sashing strips between each pair. Make three more rows the same way.

8 Measure across the centre of these rows to determine the length and cut five sashing strips (from the 5 cm wide strip) to this length. Join the four rows of blocks together, placing lengths of sashing strips between them and along the top and the bottom as well. Press.

9 Measure the length of the quilt top through the centre. Cut two sashing strips (from the 5 cm wide strip) to this length. Sew one to each side of the quilt top. Press.

12 cm

10 Measure the width of the quilt top through the centre as before to determine the length of the pieced border. Make two panels of pieced strips 12 cm wide and this length. Stitch a panel across the top and bottom of the quilt. Press.

11 Measure the length of the quilt top through the centre, including the sewn-on panels, to determine the length of the pieced side borders. Make two panels of pieced strips 12 cm wide and this length. Sew one to each side of the quilt top, taking in the edges of the pieces recently joined to the top and bottom. Press.

12 Measuring through the centre as before, cut lengths of the 5 cm wide stripping and sew them to the top and bottom of the quilt. Repeat for both sides. Press.

13 Measure the width of the quilt top through the centre and cut

two pieces of border fabric to this length and 15 cm wide. Sew them to the top and bottom of the quilt top. Repeat the procedure for the side borders. Press the quilt top carefully.

QUILTING

14 Make a template of the triangle quilting pattern opposite. Mark these triangles as shown around the border.

15 Pin-baste the batting to the wrong side of the quilt top. Place the backing fabric onto the right side of the quilt top and sew around the edges, leaving a small opening for turning. Trim the corners. Turn the quilt to the right side. Close the opening by hand. Press.

16 Pin-baste at regular intervals all over the quilt. Machine-quilt around each small square and all printed borders. Hand-quilt along the marked triangles in the plain border.

17 From the remaining length of stripping, cut twenty 5 cm squares. Press in the seam allowances on the raw edges and handsew over the junctions of the inner printed borders as shown.

TIP

The method given here is one way to complete a quilt. Another way, which you may find easier, is to assemble the three layers of the quilt and then bind the edges with a narrow strip of fabric as described in the *Single Irish Chain* quilt on page 24.

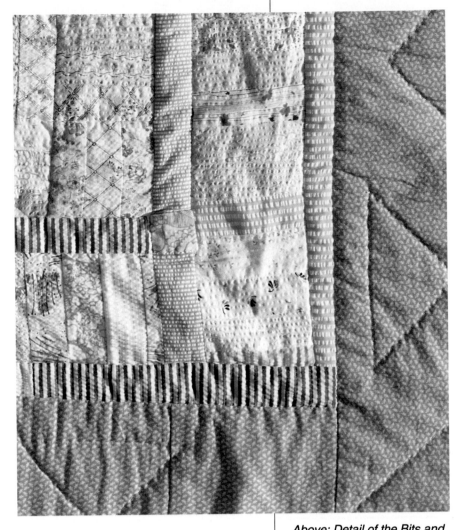

Above: Detail of the Bits and Pieces quilt showing the pieced sashes and borders

Template

STARS

Graceful hand-quilting is perfect for a simple pattern like the one in this quilt, designed and made by Dorothy Ison.

FABRIC SUGGESTIONS

A dark print and a medium print fabric have been used to define the stars on a plain cream background. Choose a third print for the border and then a plain fabric for the binding.

FINISHED SIZE

Quilt: 120 cm x 150 cm (approximately)
Block size: 30 cm x 30 cm

FABRIC QUANTITIES

1.5 m of 115 cm wide cream fabric
50 cm of 115 cm wide dark print fabric
50 cm of 115 cm wide medium print fabric
80 cm of 115 cm wide print fabric for the borders
60 cm of 115 cm wide plain fabric for binding
2.5 m of 115 cm wide fabric for backing, pieced to be 125 cm x 155 cm
125 cm x 155 cm batting

NOTIONS

*cardboard or template plastic
pencil and ruler
safety pins, pins, needles and scissors
sewing thread and quilting thread
sewing machine*

CUTTING

Do not forget to add seam allowances to each piece you cut.

1 Using the cardboard or plastic, trace and cut out the templates. For each block, cut four cream squares and one print square from template **a**; eight print triangles and eight cream triangles from template **b.**

In total, you will have six squares each in the two star prints, forty-eight cream squares, forty-eight triangles in each star print and ninety-six triangles in cream.

CONSTRUCTION

2 Chainsew the plain and print triangles together in pairs along one short side. Cut them apart. Press the seams to one side.

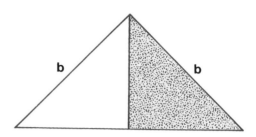

3 Join similar pairs along the long side to form a square, matching points and seams. Press.

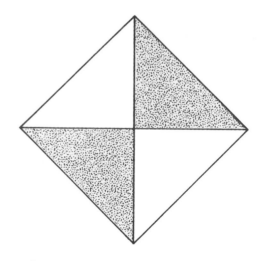

4 Taking the square just made, sew a cream square onto each coloured side. Press. Make two such strips, using the same print for each block.

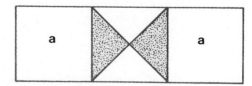

5 Sew two of the squares made in Step 3 to opposite sides of a matching print square. Press.

6 Join the pieces made in Steps 4 and 5 to make the complete block. Press. Make six blocks in each star print.

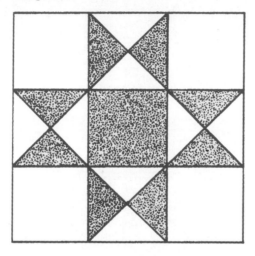

7 Join the blocks in rows of three blocks across, alternating the prints, to make the quilt top.

8 Measure the width of the quilt, measuring through the centre. Cut two strips of the border fabric to this length and 10 cm wide plus seam allowances. Sew these borders to the top and bottom of the quilt top. Measure the length of the quilt top, measuring through the centre and including the top and bottom borders. Cut two strips of the border fabric to this length and 10 cm wide plus seam allowances. Sew these to the sides of the quilt top. Press.

QUILTING

See the Pull Out Pattern Sheet at the back of the book for the quilting designs.

9 Using cardboard or template plastic, trace and cut out templates from the quilting patterns on the Pattern Sheet. Using the templates, mark the design onto the centre of each cream square and along the borders.

10 Lay the backing fabric, face down, on a table. Place the batting on top and the quilt top on top of that, face up. Baste or pin-baste all the layers together.

11 Quilt the marked designs on the cream squares and the borders. Hand-quilt along the seamlines and diagonally through the cream squares as shown.

12 Trim off any excess backing and batting.

FINISHING

13 Measure the quilt through the centre as before and cut binding fabric 10 cm wide plus seam allowances and the length of these measurements. Press the binding strips over double with wrong sides together. Place binding along the top and bottom edges of the quilt with raw edges even. Stitch the bindings in place. Repeat for the side bindings.

*Right: Detail of the
Stars quilt showing the
hand-quilting*

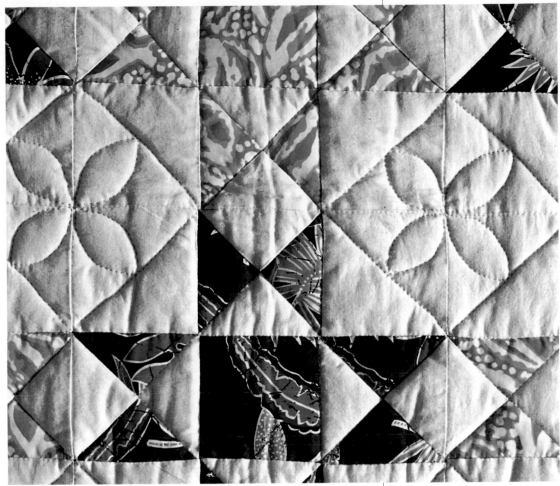

Templates

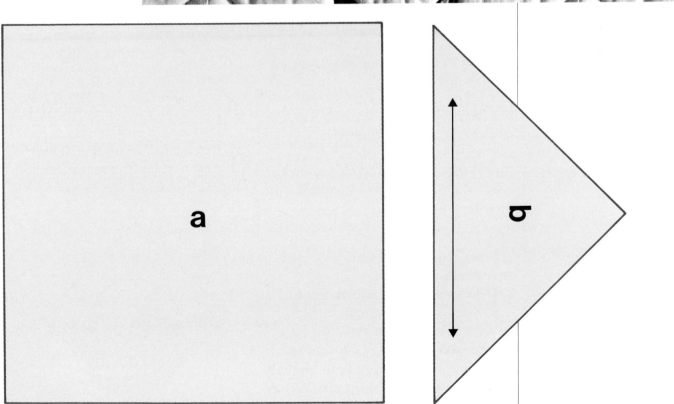

a

b

BASKET QUILT

Vicki Cordony is the proud owner of this fine example of a wonderful quilting tradition – the friendship quilt. Eight people contributed blocks to this hand-pieced and hand-quilted quilt.

FABRIC SUGGESTIONS

Various coloured cotton fabrics, utilising checks and stripes on a cream background have been used. The blocks are set on the diagonal. For the plain fabric, choose a homespun cloth and use it again for the backing.

FINISHED SIZE

Quilt: 150 cm x 176 cm
Block size: 18 cm
Total number of full blocks: 72
Total number of corner blocks: 4
Total number of border blocks: 22 half blocks

FABRIC QUANTITIES

2.5 m of 115 cm wide cotton background fabric
1.5 m of various 115 cm wide printed fabrics for the baskets
160 cm x 185 cm batting
3.2 m of cotton fabric (pieced to make 160 cm x 185 cm) for the backing
0.5 m of 115 cm wide cotton fabric for binding

NOTIONS

cardboard or template plastic
pencil and ruler
safety pins, pins, needles and scissors
sewing thread and quilting thread
sewing machine

CUTTING

Do not forget to add seam allowance to each piece you cut.

1 Cut templates **a**, **b**, **c**, **d**, and **e** from cardboard or template plastic. Lay the templates on the back of the fabric, matching grainlines on the fabric and templates. Draw around the templates with a sharp pencil. This pencil line will be the sewing line. Cut out with a 6 mm seam allowance.

2 *For each block:* Cut

template **a**	1 print
	1 plain background
template **b**	2 print
	2 plain background
template **c**	3 plain background

For the corner blocks: Cut

| template **d** | 4 plain background |

For the half blocks: Cut

| template **e** | 22 plain background |

For the handle, cut a bias strip 18 cm long and 3 cm wide from print fabric. Press in 6 mm on the raw edges on each side.

CONSTRUCTION

3 Appliqué a handle to one plain piece **a** along the dotted line with blind hem stitch. Sew the inner curve first. Press.

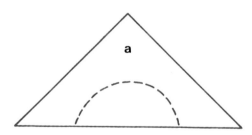

4 Join the handle triangle to the print triangle of the same size to form the handle square. Press.

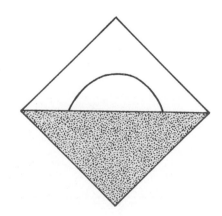

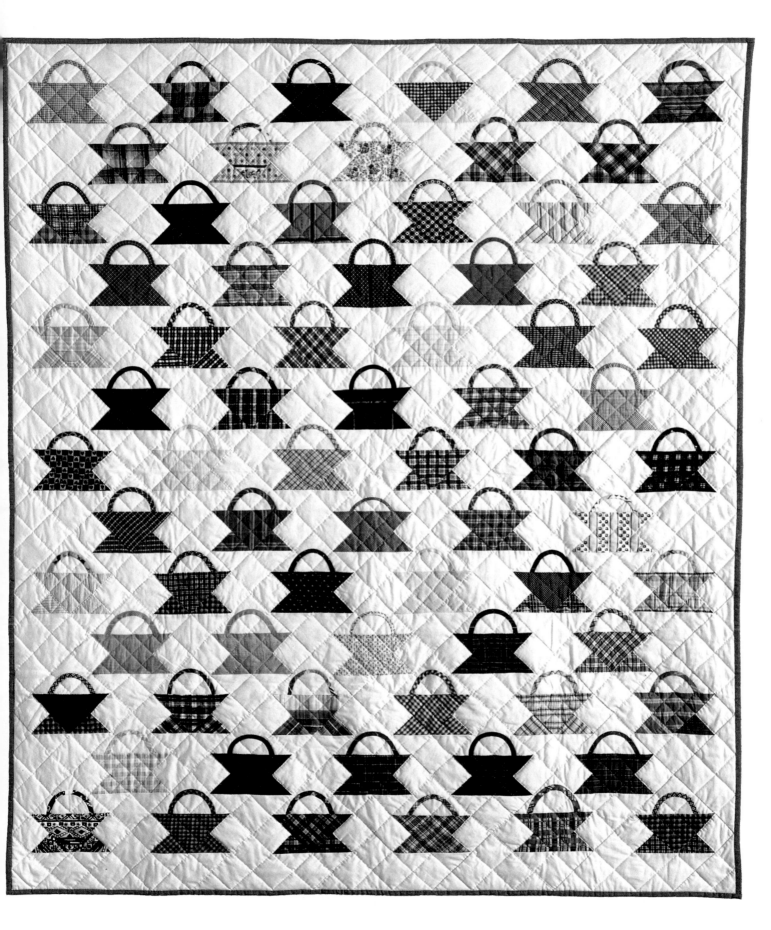

5 *To make Strip 1*: Join a print triangle **b** to a plain triangle **b** to make a square. Sew a plain square **c** to each side of the pieced square as marked. Press.

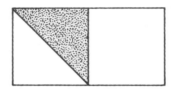

6 *To make Strip 2*: Join a print triangle **b** to a plain triangle **b** to make a square. Sew a plain square **c** to the print triangle side of this square as marked. Press.

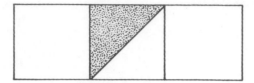

7 *To assemble the block*: Lay the handle square with the handle uppermost. Join Strip 2 to the lower right side of the handle square and Strip 1 to the lower left side, including the short end of Strip 2. Press.

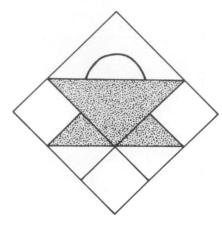

8 Lay out the 72 blocks in a pleasing colour arrangement. Join them together, adding in the corner blocks and half blocks. Press.

QUILTING

9 Lay the backing fabric face down on a table, with the batting on top. Place the pieced quilt top on top of that, face up. Smooth out any wrinkles. Baste or pin-baste through all the layers.

10 Hand-quilt the printed fabric into 2.5 cm squares. The plain fabric is quilted along the seamlines.

11 Trim off any excess backing and batting.

FINISHING

12 *For the binding*: Cut the fabric into 7 cm wide strips. Join strips together to achieve the desired lengths to bind the sides first and then the top and bottom, measuring through the centre of the quilt lengthways and widthways to determine the lengths required. Fold the strips over double with wrong sides together and raw edges even. Press. Sew the binding to the front of the quilt, with raw edges matching, and turn the pressed edge to the wrong side. Slipstitch the pressed edge to the back of the quilt.

Below: A detail of the Basket Quilt showing the diagonal quilting

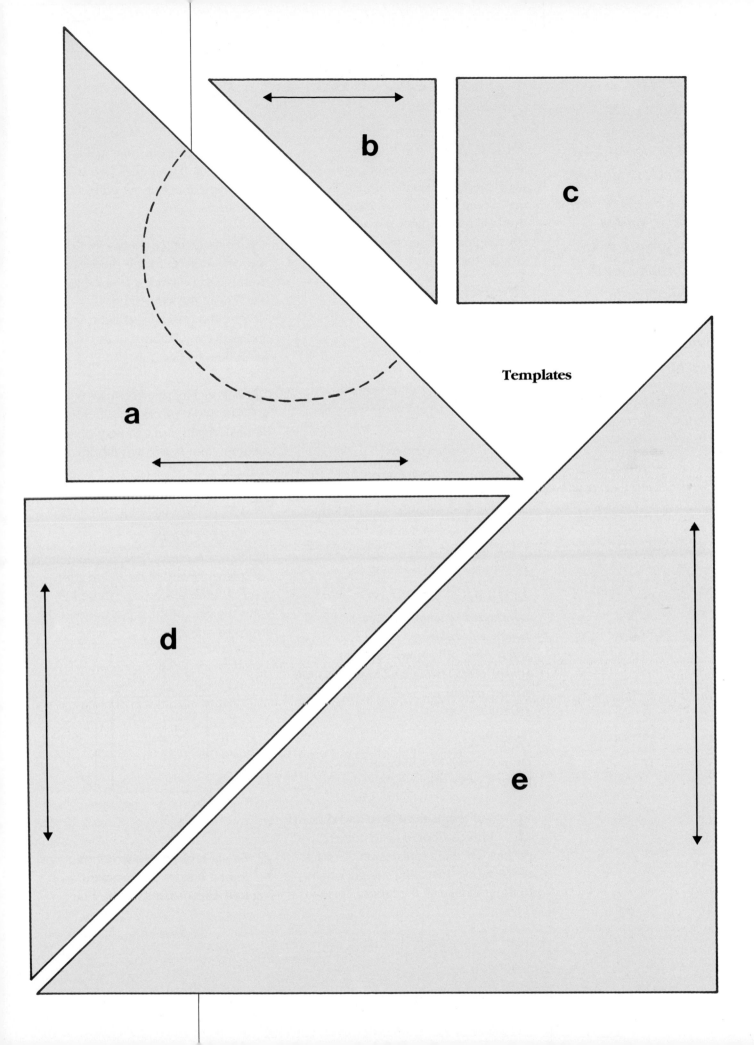

b

c

Templates

a

d

e

SQUARE-IN-SQUARE

Beryl Hodges used a multitude of 'country' fabrics in stripes and checks in muted blues, greens, reds and browns for this charming quilt, which has been machine-pieced and machine-quilted.

FABRIC SUGGESTIONS

The fabric is dress-weight cotton in light, medium and dark tones. See how some of the fabrics have been used slightly off-grain for added interest and to keep the eye moving around the quilt.

FINISHED SIZE

Quilt: 130 cm x 112 cm (approximately)
Block size: 18 cm x 18 cm
Border block size: 9 cm x 9 cm
Total number of full blocks: 30
Total number of border blocks: 48
Filler strips: 8

FABRIC QUANTITIES

20 cm each of an assortment of 115 cm wide fabric for the blocks
70 cm of 115 cm wide fabric for the borders and bindings
1.4 m of 115 cm wide backing fabric
140 cm x 120 cm wadding

NOTIONS

cardboard or template plastic
pencil and ruler
safety pins, pins, needles and scissors
rotary (Olfa) cutter and mat (optional)
sewing machine
sewing thread

CUTTING

Do not forget to add seam allowances to each piece you cut.

1 Cut templates **a**, **b**, **c** and **d** from firm cardboard or template plastic. Lay the templates on the back of the fabric, matching straight edges to the grainline of the fabric. Trace around the templates, using a soft, sharp pencil. This pencil line will be the sewing line. Cut out with seam allowances.

2 *For each of the 30 blocks:* Cut one **a** piece, four **b** pieces (each from the same fabric), four **c** pieces (each from the same fabric).

Vary the positions of light, medium and dark-toned fabrics in the blocks for added interest.

3 *For each of the 48 border blocks:* Cut two **c** pieces (in different fabrics). Again, use a variety of light, medium and dark-toned fabrics.

4 *For the filler strips:* Cut eight **d** pieces from medium-toned fabrics.

CONSTRUCTION

5 Sew a **b** piece to each side of an **a** piece. Note that the seam allowance of the **b** piece will extend beyond the side of the **a** piece. Press the seams to one side.

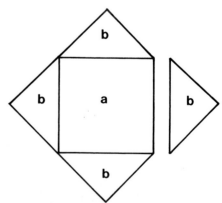

6 Sew a **c** piece to each of the joined **b** sides as illustrated on page 44. Press seams to one side.

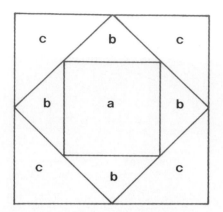

7 Lay out the thirty blocks in a pleasing colour arrangement of five rows across and six rows down.

8 Sew each row together, taking care to match the points. Press the seams to one side.

9 Sew the rows together to form the quilt top. Press the seams to one side.

10 Measure down through the centre to find the length of the quilt top. Cut two strips of border fabric the same length as this measurement, and 2.5 cm wide plus seam allowances. Join strips, if necessary, to make the length required. Sew these strips to each long side of the quilt top. Press the seams to one side.

Below: Detail of the quilt

11 Measure across through the centre to find the width of the quilt, including the border strips. Cut two strips of border fabric the same length as this measurement, and 2.5 cm wide plus seam allowances. Join strips, if necessary, to make the length required. Sew these strips to the short sides of the quilt top. Press the seams to one side.

12 Piece the border block by sewing two **c** blocks together. Press the seams to one side. Lay out the forty-eight border blocks around the quilt top, taking account of the tonal values and changing the angle of the seam in alternate blocks.

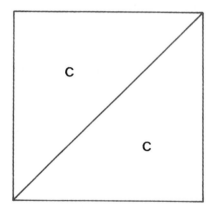

13 Place the filler strips around the corner blocks as illustrated. Join the border blocks into rows with the filler strips and stitch them to the sides of the quilt top. Press quilt top well.

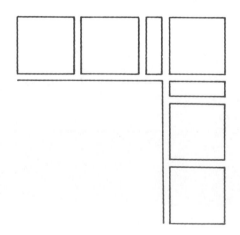

QUILTING

14 Assemble the three layers on a flat surface, placing the backing fabric first face down, then the wadding, and finally the quilt top with right side up. Smooth out any wrinkles. Pin-baste the three layers together well with safety pins.

15 Quilt by machine along the seamlines.

FINISHING

16 Trim off any excess wadding and backing fabric. Cut two lengths of binding fabric 8 cm wide for the quilt sides and two lengths for the top and bottom. Measure, as before, through the centre of the quilt to determine the lengths. Press the strips over double with wrong sides together. Place the binding on the right side of the quilt with raw edges even. Stitch in a 1 cm seam. Turn the binding to the wrong side and slipstitch into place.

17 Embroider your name and the date on your quilt.

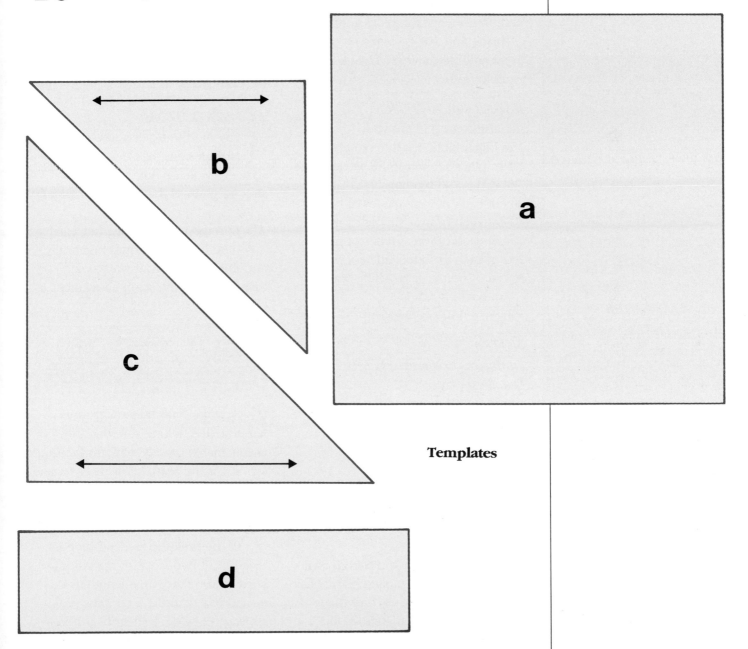

Templates

TRIANGLE WALL QUILT

Colour is crucial in this dazzling quilt, designed and made by Beryl Hodges. This quilt has been machine-pieced and machine-quilted.

Right: The quilt is pictured hanging vertically. To follow the construction instructions, turn the page sideways.

FABRIC SUGGESTIONS

Having decided on your four colours to contrast with the black, choose four toning shades of each one. You can use both print and plain cotton dress fabrics as long as the tones are right.

FINISHED SIZE

Quilt: 147 cm x 105 cm (approximately)
Block size: 10 cm triangle
Total number of full blocks: 207 (103 black and 104 coloured)
Total half blocks: 18 (10 black and 8 coloured)

FABRIC QUANTITIES

All fabrics are 115 cm wide
1 m black fabric for the triangles
1.3 m black fabric for the second border and bindings
20 cm each of four shades of blue
20 cm each of four shades of pink
20 cm each of four shades of green
20 cm each of four shades of purple
30 cm of border fabric (first border)
1.5 m backing fabric
150 cm x 110 cm wadding

NOTIONS

cardboard or template plastic
pencil and ruler
rotary (Olfa) cutter and mat
safety pins, pins, needles and scissors
sewing machine
sewing thread

CUTTING

Do not forget to add seam allowances to each piece you cut.

1 Cut templates **a** and **b** from firm cardboard or template plastic. Lay the templates on the back of the fabric, with base of triangle along grainline of fabric. Trace around the template using a firm, sharp pencil. This pencil line will be the sewing line. Cut out with seam allowances.

2 Using template **a**, cut: one hundred and three black triangles and one hundred and four coloured triangles in the required numbers for each shade as shown.

3 Using template **b**, cut: ten black half triangles, and eight coloured half triangles in the required numbers for each shade as shown.

CONSTRUCTION

4 Lay out the black and coloured triangles and half triangles in the correct colour layout, placing the straight grain of the fabric horizontally.

5 Join the triangles together into nine horizontal rows, beginning and ending each row with a half triangle. Press the seam allowances to one side.

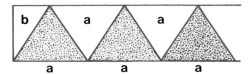

6 Sew the nine horizontal rows together, taking care that the points match exactly, to form the quilt top. Press the seam allowances to one side.

7 Measure down through the centre of the quilt top to determine its length. Cut two strips of the coloured border fabric the same length as this measurement and 2.5 cm plus seam allowances wide. Join strips if neces-

sary to achieve the length required. Sew these strips to each short side of the quilt top, taking care to sew exactly at the points of the triangles.

8 Measure across through the centre of the quilt top, including the border strips, to find the width. Cut two strips of coloured border fabric as for the side borders and attach in the same way.

9 Repeat steps 7 and 8 for the black border, cutting the strips 10 cm wide plus seam allowances. Press the quilt top carefully.

10 Assemble the layers of the quilt on a table with the backing facing down, the wadding in between and the quilt top facing upwards. Baste with big stitches or pin-baste through all thicknesses to secure the three layers of the quilt together.

QUILTING

11 Machine-quilt in the seamlines of the triangles and borders, taking the quilting stitching through the borders all the way to the edges.

FINISHING

12 Trim off excess wadding and backing. Cut two lengths of 8 cm wide black binding for the quilt sides and two lengths for the quilt top and bottom. Measure through the centres, as before, to determine the lengths. Press the strips over double with wrong sides together. Place the binding on the right side of the quilt with raw edges even. Stitch. Turn the binding to the wrong side and slipstitch into place.

13 Sew a sleeve along the top of the quilt back, so that a light batten can be threaded through for hanging. Sign and date your quilt.

Right: Detail of the Triangle Wall Quilt showing the borders and the diagonal quilting

CARE OF QUILTS

Look after your quilt and it will last long enough to become a family heirloom. The enemies are dust, light, humidity and insects. Good housekeeping will help to preserve your quilt and protect it from damage.

Cotton quilts should be washed in your washing machine on a gentle cycle, in warm water, and dried flat in the shade. Quilts should not be exposed to strong light. If you need to store a quilt for long periods, take it out regularly for airing every six months and then fold it in a different way before putting it back into store.

The correct way to fold a quilt when it is not in use, is to fold it with the right side outwards. Then put it into a bag made of well-washed cotton fabric along with rolls of acid-free tissue paper, tucked into the folds. Never store a quilt in a plastic bag as this traps humidity in the enclosed air and causes discoloration. The cotton bag, with the quilt inside, can be put into a cardboard box with mothballs outside the bag to discourage insects.

Most important of all, your quilt was made to be enjoyed for its usefulness and admired for its beauty.

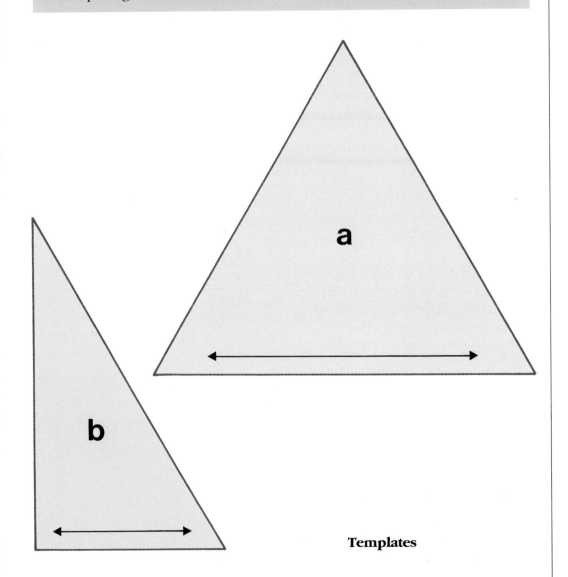

Templates

FLYING GEESE

In this traditional quilt, designed and made by Ann Crafter, the pattern works in parallel lines of triangles along the length of the quilt. It is not difficult to imagine that the triangles are in fact geese flying in formation, with outstretched wings.

FABRIC SUGGESTIONS

The 'sky' triangles are often white or cream and the 'geese' are either in a combination of toning colours and fabrics (as in this quilt) or in a single contrasting colour. For our quilt we have chosen six different fabrics for the 'geese' – two light, two medium and two dark. The interesting striped sashes are not pieced but are in fact cut from a striped fabric which gives the effect of being pieced from a number of different stripes.

This quilt is machine-pieced and machine-quilted.

Seam allowances of 6 mm have been included.

FINISHED SIZE

Quilt: 124 cm x 103 cm (approximately)
Block size: 18 cm x 9 cm
Total number of full blocks: 30

FABRIC QUANTITIES

6 different scrap fabrics for the geese
All the following fabrics are 115 cm wide:
80 cm light colour for the background
   paisley striped fabric for the sashes
50 cm dark plain colour for border
40 cm contrasting plain fabric for
   binding
130 cm x 115 m plain fabric for backing
130 cm x 110 cm batting

NOTIONS

cardboard or template plastic
pencil and ruler
rotary (Olfa) cutter and mat
safety pins, pins, needles and scissors
sewing thread
sewing machine

CUTTING

1 Cut 11.5 cm wide strips from the six colours of scrap fabric and 11.5 cm strips from the light background colour. Cut these into 11.5 cm lengths to make squares.

2 Cut four sashes from the striped fabric to be approximately 9 cm wide and 91.5 cm long.

CONSTRUCTION

3 Place one background square and one print square together with right sides facing and draw a line diagonally from one corner to the other. Sew a line of stitching 6 mm on either side of this line.

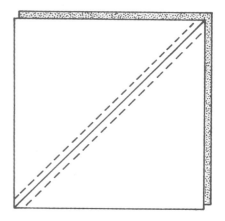

4 Cut along the pencil line, open out the fabric and you will have

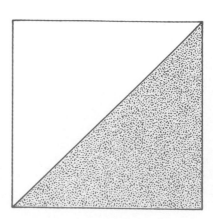

two new squares half 'goose' and half background. Sew the 'goose' sides of the squares together, matching print fabrics, to make a rectangular block. Press. Make five of these blocks in each print fabric, making a total of thirty blocks.

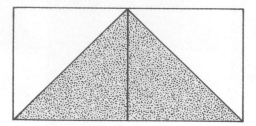

5 Lay the rectangles out in three rows of ten so that you can judge the arrangement of colours and prints. Sew them into three strips. Make sure that the geese are 'flying' in the same direction across the quilt when the strips are laid next to each other. Press.

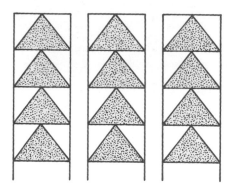

6 Join the three 'geese' strips with striped sashes in between and on the outside, making sure the rectangles are in line. The sashes on the outside form the inner border. Measure across the centre to find the width of the quilt top. Cut two sashes to this width. Sew them to the top and bottom of the quilt top. Press.

7 Measure down the centre of the quilt to find the full length. Cut two outside borders from the plain, dark fabric of this length and 9.5 cm

wide. Sew them to the sides of the quilt. Measure through the centre of the quilt top, including the borders just attached, to find the full width. Cut two outer borders to this length and 9.5 cm wide. Sew them to the top and bottom of the quilt top. Press the quilt top carefully.

8 Cut the backing fabric to size and place it right side down. If you can fit it on a table, sticky tape it to the table to stop it from slipping. Place the batting over the backing and the pieced quilt top over this, with the right side up. Smooth out any wrinkles and, using safety pins, pin the three layers together all over the quilt.

QUILTING

9 Starting in the middle of the quilt (using a walking foot, if you have one) stitch around the 'geese' triangles first.

TIP

It's a good idea to do the quilting in zigzag lines, working down only one side of each 'goose' from top to bottom, and then stitching the other side from top to bottom. This means you can work in continuous rows without too much starting and stopping in your sewing.

10 Stitch across the striped borders with parallel rows of stitching, approximately 3 cm apart. Take care to mark this out first so you end up with even rows at the corners. The plain dark border and the sashes are quilted in with joined ovals, the pattern for which is given opposite. Trace the design and make a template for your stitching. Transfer the design to your fabric, using a silver pencil or a water-soluble pencil. Trim off any excess backing and batting.

FINISHING

11 Measure through the centre of the quilt lengthways and crossways as before to determine the lengths of the binding strips. Cut the binding to be 8 cm wide. Press the binding strips over double with wrong sides together. Stitch the binding to the right side of the quilt with raw edges even. Turn the binding to the wrong side of the quilt and handsew it into place.

Above: Detail of quilt showing the border, sashes and quilting

Quilting design

EVENING STAR

Designed and made by Lee Cleland, this large quilt is made up of two blocks, Evening Star and Dutch Tile. This quilt has been machine-pieced and machine-quilted.

FABRIC SUGGESTIONS

Choose a light fabric for the background of the stars; a medium one for the triangles of the Dutch Tile block and side triangles; a medium to dark fabric for the points of the star, the centre square of Dutch Tile and the first border; choose a darker fabric for the centre of the star and the outside border. The blocks are set diagonally.

FINISHED SIZE

Quilt: 210 cm x 250 cm
Block size: 25.5 cm
Total number of full blocks:
    30 Evening Star
    20 Dutch Tile

FABRIC QUANTITIES

All fabrics are 115 cm wide.
3 m light fabric
2.5 m medium fabric
3.7 m medium to dark fabric
2.6 m dark fabric
220 cm x 260 cm backing fabric
    (pieced from 5.2 m of 115 cm
    wide fabric)
220 cm x 260 cm wadding

NOTIONS

cardboard or template plastic
water-soluble pencil or silver pencil
ruler
tracing paper
rotary (Olfa) cutter and mat (optional)
safety pins, needles and scissors
sewing thread
sewing machine

CUTTING

See the Pull Out Pattern Sheet for the templates. Do not forget to add seam allowances to all the pieces you cut out except for the side triangles which already include 6 mm seam allowances.

1 Make templates **1a**, **1b**, **1c**, **2a**, **2b**, **2c** from cardboard. Using a sharp pencil, trace around the templates on the wrong side of the fabric. Cut them out, adding seam allowances. The pencil line will be your sewing line. Cut the pieces for the blocks along the length of the fabric to allow you to cut the borders along the length later.

For the Dutch Tile block: Cut,
20 squares (template **1a**) medium to dark fabric
80 triangles (template **2a**) medium fabric

For the Evening Star block: Cut,
30 squares (template **1b**) dark fabric
240 triangles (template **2c**) medium to dark fabric
120 triangles (template **2b**) light fabric
120 squares (template **1c**) light fabric

For the side triangles: Cut five 39 cm squares of light fabric and cut them diagonally through the centre into four triangles.
NOTE: These side triangles *include* seam allowances.

For the corner triangles: Cut four of template **2d** of light fabric.

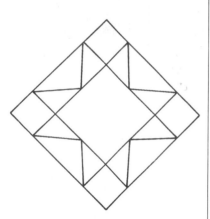

Evening Star block

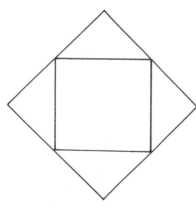

Dutch Tile block

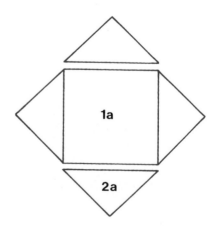

54

CONSTRUCTION

For the Dutch Tile blocks:

2 Join the long side of a triangle **2a** to each side of the square **1a** in a 6 mm seam. Press this and all following seams to one side.

For the Evening Star blocks:

3 Join a triangle **2c** to each short side of a triangle **2b** to form Strip 1. Press.

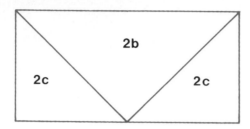

4 Sew a Strip 1 to two opposite sides of a square **1b**. Press.

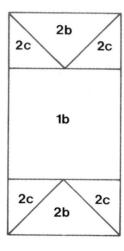

5 Make two more Strip 1 pieces. On each one, join a square **1c** to the other short side of the triangle **2c** to form Strip 2. Press.

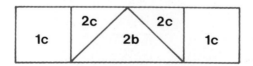

6 Sew a Strip 2 to opposite sides of the square **1b** to complete the block. Press.

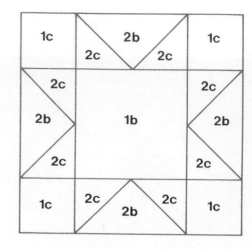

7 Join the blocks diagonally, alternating rows of Dutch Tile and Evening Star blocks. Sew the corner and side triangles into place.

8 *For the borders:* Measure the width of the quilt top through the centre and then the length through the centre (allowing for the width of the top and bottom borders) to find the length required for the borders. Add an extra 40 cm to each one to allow for the mitred corners. From the medium to dark fabric, cut the strips for the inner border 7 cm wide plus seam allowances. From the dark fabric, cut strips for the second border 10 cm wide plus seam allowances. Sew both strips together for each border, making a wide, striped border. Sew these to the top, bottom and sides of the quilt, stopping the stitching short of the seam allowances of the quilt top at the corners. Fold the quilt at the corners, so that the edges of the borders are matching and stitch the corners of the borders together in a line with the fold in the quilt to form a mitred corner.

9 Trace the quilting patterns from the pattern sheet. Make a template from the cardboard or plastic. Using the template, a silver pencil or water-soluble pencil, draw the designs onto the quilt top. Use the circle for the

Dutch Tile blocks, the flower for the centre square of the *Evening Star* block, the corner triangles and the side triangles, and the border pattern, including the corner pattern, for the quilt border.

10 Place the three layers of the quilt together – backing right side facing down, wadding on top and then the quilt top with the right side up. Pin-baste through all thicknesses.

QUILTING

See the Pull Out Pattern Sheet for the quilting designs.

11 Quilt by machine along the pattern lines.

FINISHING

12 *For the binding:* Cut two lengths of dark fabric 8 cm wide plus seam allowances for the quilt sides and two lengths the same width for the top and bottom. Measure through the centre of the quilt as before to determine the lengths of binding required. Press the binding over double with wrong sides together and raw edges even. Lay the binding on the right side of the quilt with raw edges together and stitch in a 1 cm seam. Fold the pressed edge to the wrong side and slipstitch into place.

Left: Detail of the Evening Star quilt showing the dainty quilting designs

GARDEN PATH

Lynette McKinley, designer and quiltmaker, chose a lush floral print to combine with a strong geometric pattern. The quilt has been machine-pieced and machine-quilted.

FABRIC SUGGESTIONS

For added interest, the floral design works in striped panels and the triangular template **c** has been cut from different parts of the stripe. This process does involve a lot of wastage so you will need to be generous when buying fabric. The quilt, which has been made using six each of two blocks, can be enlarged by adding more blocks.

6 mm seam allowances are included.

FINISHED SIZE

Quilt: 119 cm x 150 cm (approximately)
Block size: 31 cm square
Total number of full blocks: 12

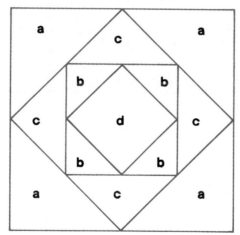

Block 1

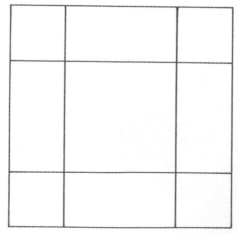

Block 2

FABRIC QUANTITIES

1 m (approximately) of striped floral fabric
60 cm blue fabric for small triangles
70 cm cream fabric for large triangles and blocks
20 cm red print fabric
40 cm plain red fabric
1.6 m striped fabric for borders
3.1 m of 115 cm wide backing fabric pieced to make 125 cm x 155 cm (if you have a crossways seam in the backing you can reduce this to 2.5 m)
125 cm x 155 cm batting

NOTIONS

template plastic
pencil and ruler
rotary (Olfa) cutter and mat
safety pins, pins, needles and scissors
sewing thread and quilting thread
(This quilt has been quilted with invisible thread.)
sewing machine

CUTTING

See the Pull Out Pattern Sheet for the templates.
For Block 1:

1 Cut the four templates out of transparent plastic so you can plan the placement of the fabric pattern. Cut template **d** six times out of the centre roses, placing each one the same way on the fabric.

2 Fold the blue fabric in half and then fold it again so you have four layers. After straightening the edge and

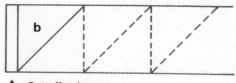

↑ *Cut off selvage*

cutting off the selvages, cut a strip 10 cm wide using scissors or, preferably, a rotary cutter and plastic ruler. Lay template **b** along the strip as shown and cut out twenty-four triangles.

3 The next triangles, **c**, are cut individually from the striped material. Lay the see-through template down over a particular stripe and cut four triangles the same from each section for each of the six blocks.

4 From the cream fabric, cut two strips across the width of the fabric each 17 cm wide. Cut twenty-four triangles from the cream fabric using template **a**.

For Block 2:

5 Folding the fabric into four as for the blue fabric, cut two 9 cm wide strips across the width of the floral fabric. Cut one 16.5 cm wide strip across the plain cream fabric. Cut two 9 cm wide and one 16.5 cm wide strips from the plain red fabric.

CONSTRUCTION

6 *To make Block 1:* Sew the long side of a blue triangle to all four sides of the small floral square cut

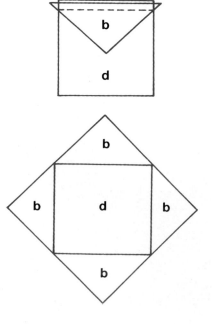

from template **d**. They should extend beyond the corners of the square to enable the next triangle to go on without losing the point of the square.

7 Join four striped triangles to the sides of the square and then sew on four plain cream triangles. Make five more of these blocks. Press all the blocks carefully.

8 *To make Block 2:* Join the two floral strips across their width with the one 16.5 cm wide plain red strip in between.

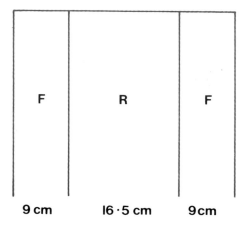

9 Press the seams to one side and cut the joined strip into strips 9 cm wide.

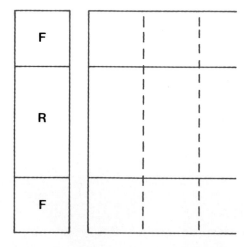

10 Join a 9 cm wide strip of plain red to each long side of the 16.5 cm plain cream strip. Press the seams to one side and cut into strips

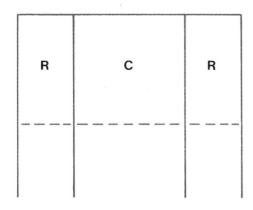

| R | C | R |

16.5 cm wide. Piece two strips with the floral squares on both ends to two opposite sides of the plain red and cream strip. Make five more of these blocks. Press all blocks carefully.

F	R	F
R	C	R
F	R	F

11 Piece the quilt together, alternating blocks and matching corners carefully. Sew in rows, first Block 1, then Block 2, then Block 1. In the second row, join Block 2, Block 1, then Block 2. For the third row, join Block 1, then Block 2, then Block 1 and so on. Continue until the quilt is finished.

12 Measure the width of the quilt through the centre. Cut the border from the striped fabric to this length, using whatever width best complements your stripes. Join the borders to the top and bottom of the quilt. Press. Repeat for the border on the sides of the quilt.

QUILTING

13 Place the backing fabric face down on a table and sticky tape it to the table to prevent it slipping. Place the batting on top and then the pieced quilt top on top of that, face up. Carefully smooth out all the wrinkles. Using large safety pins and starting in the middle of the quilt, pin all three layers together. Machine-quilt, or hand-quilt if you prefer, the complete top with criss-crossing diagonal rows of stitching, about 6 cm apart. Trim off any excess backing and batting.

FINISHING

14 Cut 8 cm wide strips from the plain red fabric for the binding. Measure across the centre of the quilt to find the length and width to calculate the length of binding required. The edges of a quilt are sometimes stretched and it may ripple along the edges and not sit straight, making accurate measurement a problem. Fold the binding strip over double with wrong sides together and raw edges matching. Sew to the top and bottom edges of the quilt, stretching the binding to fit along the edges. Sew the rest to both sides of the quilt. Turn to the back of the quilt and handsew in place.

KEY		
R	=	RED
C	=	CREAM
F	=	FLORAL

Below: Detail of the Garden Path quilt showing the criss-crossing machine quillting

SEMINOLE MOUNTAIN

This charming quilt, designed and made by Sandy Mann, is a combination of traditional quilting designs. It is very important, to measure and cut this quilt accurately, and to be accurate with the 1 cm seam allowance.

FABRIC SUGGESTIONS

Seminole patterns involve joining strips of patches, often in very bright colours, which are then cut up before being joined into new combinations. This quilt is made by the chain sewing method which is a great time saver.

FINISHED SIZE

Quilt: 154 cm x 96 cm
Squares: 6 cm

FABRIC QUANTITIES

90 cm of 115 cm wide green print
    fabric
70 cm of 115 cm wide cream print
    fabric
20 cm of 115 cm wide coral print
    fabric
80 cm of 115 cm plain cream fabric
65 cm plain coral fabric for borders
1.6 m x 45 cm plain coral backing
    fabric
160 cm x 115 cm batting

NOTIONS

cardboard or template plastic
pencils and ruler
rotary (Olfa) cutter and mat
safety pins, pins, needles and scissors
sewing thread
sewing machine

CUTTING

1 The triangular template includes seam allowances. Use it to cut out in the following quantities: 130 green print, 146 cream print, 24 coral print.

2 Cut three 8 cm wide strips of green print and six 8 cm wide strips of plain coral for the Seminole strips.

3 Before cutting the borders, it is best to measure the length and width of the main panel, measuring through the centre. Join fabric as necessary to achieve the lengths required for border strips.

CONSTRUCTION

4 Chainsew the following combination of triangles together into squares. Do not cut them apart, but feed in one pair of patches after another and sew them all at once. 8 green print triangles into 4 squares 124 green print triangles and 124 cream print triangles into 124 squares; 24 coral print triangles and 24 cream print triangles into 24 squares. Cut the threads between patches and press the seams to one side.

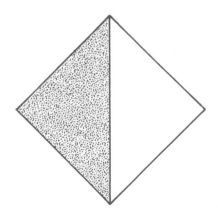

5 Sew the squares into strips following the diagram provided on the next page, for placement of the various colours. It is important when sewing the joined patches together, to match the cross seams. Pin them together as shown, stitch and press the seams to one side. Continue in this manner.

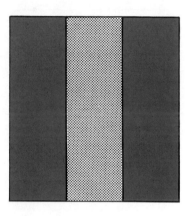

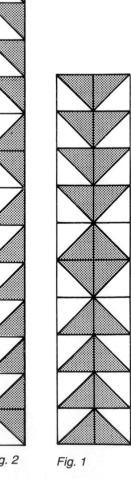

Fig. 2   Fig. 1

centre. Join them to the side edges of the panel. (Fig. 2)

10 Measure the quilt top as in Step 6 and cut and attach the 8 cm wide cream and coral plain borders as for the inner borders, sewing the top and bottom borders first and then the sides.

11 *For the Seminole strips:* Join the green print strips between two plain coral strips. Press the seams open. Cut the joined strip into 8 cm lengths.

Pin and sew the lengths together in an offset pattern as shown in the diagram below. Press the seams open. Trim diagonally through the coral squares, allowing for seam allowances.

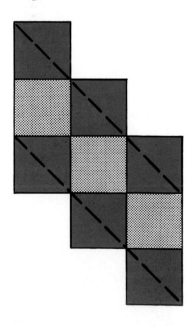

6 Measure the width of the panel through the centre and cut two plain coral borders 4.5 cm wide and as long as this length. Sew these strips to the top and bottom of the centre panel. Measure the length of the quilt, including the coral border, and cut two 4.5 cm wide plain coral borders for the sides. Sew them to both sides of the centre panel.

7 Measure the quilt top as in Step 6. Cut and sew 5.5 cm wide plain cream borders for the top, bottom and sides.

8 Make four strips, each with ten green and cream print squares, noting that the direction of the seams changes in the centre. Join two strips together and join them to the top and bottom edges of the panel. (Fig. 1)

9 Make two strips, each with sixteen green and cream print squares, noting the change of direction of the seams at the ends and in the

12 Measure the width of the quilt top through the centre. Sew the Seminole strips of this measurement to the top and bottom of the quilt.

13 Measure the width of the quilt top through the centre and cut and add another 8 cm cream border to the top and bottom of the quilt. Press the quilt top carefully.

QUILTING

14 Pencil mark your quilting design on the borders, meeting edges and points where possible.

15 Assemble quilt layers, placing the backing face down on a table, then the batting and finally the quilt top, face up. Pin-baste together with safety pins. Machine-quilt along seamlines and in the marked pattern on the borders.

16 *For the mock binding*: Machine sew or tack around the edge of the quilt. Trim the wadding around the edges. Trim the backing to be 2.5 cm wider all around each edge.

17 Fold the corner of the backing in half and then over again onto the top of the quilt. Press under the raw edge of the binding all around the quilt and fold the edge onto the front of the quilt. Pin the binding in place, folding in and cutting away the excess fabric at the corners, forming mitred corners. Slipstitch the corners closed. Stitch the folded edge of the binding down onto the quilt front.

Above: Detail of the Seminole Mountain quilt showing the pieced borders

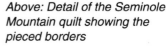

KEY

= YELLOW

= GREEN

= CORAL

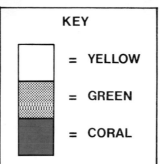

Template

Quick Quilts

The passing of time changes everything, and perhaps nowhere more than in the way homes are furnished with individual creativity. The very best traditional ideas and techniques are shown here, adapted for contemporary projects. They're all simple to make, effective, pretty and practical.

SILK NURSERY QUILT

This delightful nursery quilt is as soft as silk. The pretty nursery designs were first painted by Annie Ubeda, then the quilt was machine-sewn and machine-quilted by Martina Oprey.

FABRIC SUGGESTIONS

Silk is the only suitable fabric for this lovely quilt, given the specialised painting technique. You could also use a cotton fabric and paint it with acrylic fabric paints. This quilt is backed with a striped cotton fabric which should be pre-washed.

FINISHED SIZE

Quilt: 1 m square

FABRIC QUANTITIES

1 m square pure silk Habutai
1.1 m square cotton or silk for backing
1.1 m square polyester batting

NOTIONS AND PAINTS

paint colours from Orient Express
   Pebeo: Orange No. 25; Yellow No. 63;
   Night Bleu No. 55; China Bleu No. 3;
   Green Gold No. 17; Moss Green No.
   43; Grey No. 47; Red Turquish No. 31
soft, washable pencil
adhesive tape
large wooden frame of the size of the
   silk to be painted
push pins, safety pins
clear gutta
gutta applicator and nib 7
Squirrel brush: sizes 4, 8, 10
   and 12
Orient Express fixative
sewing machine

PAINTING METHOD

See the Pull Out Pattern Sheet for the motif outlines.

1 Mark the silk with a washable pencil so that you have nine 22.5 cm squares separated by borders that are 6.5 cm wide. The outer border will start wider but will be the same width when the quilt is bound.

2 Locate the motifs on the Pattern Sheet. Centre the marked squares over the motifs and trace off the designs using a soft lead pencil. The silk is so transparent that the design will easily be seen through it. Use adhesive tape to hold the silk in place.

3 Stretch the silk onto the wooden frame, securing it with push pins and making sure that the silk is taut. Draw over the pencil tracing with the gutta applicator. This forms a barrier, keeping the colour in the area where it is intended to be. Do this carefully, without leaving any gaps. A broken line will allow the colour to run through. Gutta dries very quickly, so you do not have to wait too long before you start painting.

4 The paint has been diluted up to ten times with water to obtain these pastel tones. The blue has been mixed with a touch of grey and the teddy bear coloured with a mix of red and grey. The duck is painted with yellow and orange. These colours are just a guide. Use your own colours if you wish, then paint the borders to complement them.

5 Leave the silk to dry for forty-eight hours. Prepare the solution of fixative and water as directed on the bottle of fixative. Dip the whole piece of silk in the solution for ten minutes, then wring it out and rinse it in clean water. Do not worry about the amount of colour that runs out. Keep the fixative, as it can be used several times. Iron while it is still damp.

CONSTRUCTION

6 Place the backing fabric face down on a table. Tape it to the table to keep it from slipping. Place the batting on top and then the painted silk, face up. Baste these three layers together.

QUILTING

7 Machine-quilt along the painted border lines as shown.

FINISHING

8 When the quilting is complete, trim away any excess batting and silk, 1 cm from the outer stitching, leaving the backing fabric protruding. Trim the backing fabric so that it is 3 cm wider all round than the quilt top.

9 Bring the backing fabric border over the edge of the silk, turning under 1 cm at the raw edge. Fold in the corners at right angles to create false mitres. Stitch the folded edge of the false binding 6.5 cm from the edge of the outer painted border.

Magic Quilt

This magic quilt folds up and tucks into a sewn-on pocket, making a pillow! Every sofa needs pillows and something warm to snuggle into – how convenient to unwrap the pillow and find a cuddly quilt inside!

FABRIC SUGGESTIONS

We have chosen pre-printed cushion panels, with one extra panel for the sewn-on pocket into which the quilt folds away. For a different look, make the quilt from an all-over print, plain fabric, or piece one from a number of different fabrics. Remember that the pocket on the back of the quilt needs to have at least one side in the same fabric as the quilt back.

FINISHED SIZE

Quilt: 1.18 m x 1.62 m
Pocket: 45 cm x 45 cm

FABRIC QUANTITIES

1.7 m of 120 cm wide fabric for the quilt top
1.7 m of 1.2 cm wide fabric for the quilt back
46 cm x 50 cm for each side of the pocket
170 cm x 130 cm quilter's batting for the quilt
45 cm x 45 cm quilter's batting for the pillow

NOTIONS

sewing thread
safety pins, pins
sewing machine

CUTTING

1 cm allowances are included in the cutting instructions

1 Cut out one quilt front, one quilt back and two pocket pieces in the sizes given.

CONSTRUCTION

2 With the right side facing upwards, place the quilt front over the batting. Pin-baste to secure.

3 With the right side facing upwards, place the pocket front over the batting. Pin-baste to secure. Place the pocket back over the front, with right sides together. Stitch around all the edges in a 1 cm seam, leaving an opening for turning.

4 Turn the pocket to the right side and handsew the opening closed. Press. Machine-quilt through all thicknesses, following any lines on the front you wish to emphasise.

5 Place the pocket on the back of the quilt in the centre of one short end, 1 cm in from the end. Stitch the pillow in place around three sides, with the opening facing the middle of the quilt. If you have used two coordinating fabrics, make sure the fabric that matches the back is facing upwards when you are positioning the pocket.

6 Place the quilt back over the quilt front, with right sides facing. Stitch around all the edges, leaving an opening for turning.

7 Turn the quilt to the right side and press. Handsew the opening closed. Tie the quilt through all the layers, where the 'blocks' intersect.

Above right: The magic quilt opened out
Right: Hand-quilt around the motifs for a different look
Far right: Use a coordinating print to frame the pillow piece before sewing. The magic quilt folds into the pillow

To fold the quilt: Place the quilt with the pocket facing downwards and fold in both sides to cross over in the middle. Beginning at the end with no pocket, fold the quilt in pocket-sized lengths up to the pocket. Bring the pocket from the back to the front, turning it to contain the quilt as you go.

PILLOW QUILT

Tonia Todman designed the arrangement of colours and patterns for this quilt. The quilt can be any size you like, depending on the number and size of the squares. Martina Oprey used an overlocker to join the squares together and speed up construction.

FABRIC SUGGESTIONS

The construction method of this quilt lends itself to creating a design using different related fabrics. We've chosen a range of prints in blue and white, but this quilt would be just as eye-catching using plain fabrics in pastels or primary colours. It could even become a 'memory' quilt by using scraps from the children's clothes or your favourite dresses. Experiment with stripes and checks, mixed with floral prints.

FINISHED SIZE

Quilt: 1.62 m x 1.98 m
Square size: 18 cm

FABRIC QUANTITIES

3.6 m of 115 cm wide fabric for fabric 1
1 m of 115 cm wide fabric for fabric 2
3.6 m of 115 cm wide fabric for fabric 3
80 cm of 115 cm wide fabric for fabric 4

NOTIONS

polyester fibre stuffing
sewing thread
pins
sewing machine or overlocker

CUTTING

1 cm seam allowances are included in the cutting instructions

1 Cut 20 cm x 20 cm squares in the following quantities:
88 squares from fabric 1
24 squares from fabric 2
70 squares from fabric 3
16 squares from fabric 4

CONSTRUCTION

2 Place the squares of identical fabric together in pairs with right sides facing. Overlock or stitch around three sides to form the pillows, leaving the remaining side open.

3 Turn the pillows to the right side and push out the corners neatly. Press them flat, pressing the seams carefully.

4 Turn in 1 cm on both edges of the open side of each pillow and press.

5 Place the squares in horizontal rows as directed below, working from the top left corner of the quilt.

Row 1: 9 pillows of fabric 1
Row 2: 1 pillow of fabric 1, 7 pillows of fabric 3, 1 pillow of fabric 1
Row 3: 1 pillow of fabric 1, 3 pillows of fabric 3, 1 pillow of fabric 2, 3 pillows of fabric 3, 1 pillow of fabric 1
Row 4: 1 pillow of fabric 1, 2 pillows of fabric 3, 1 pillow of fabric 2, 1 pillow of fabric 4, 1 pillow of fabric 2, 2 pillows of fabric 3, 1 pillow of fabric 1
Row 5: 1 pillow of fabric 1, 1 pillow of fabric 3, 1 pillow of fabric 2, 1 pillow of fabric 4, 1 pillow of fabric 1, 1 pillow of fabric 4, 1 pillow of fabric 2, 1 pillow of fabric 3, 1 pillow of fabric 1
Row 6: 1 pillow of fabric 1, 1 pillow of fabric 2, 1 pillow of fabric 4, 1 pillow of fabric 1, 1 pillow of fabric 3, 1 pillow of fabric 1, 1 pillow of fabric 4, 1 pillow of fabric 2, 1 pillow of fabric 1

Row 7: 1 pillow of fabric 1, 1 pillow of fabric 3, 1 pillow of fabric 2, 1 pillow of fabric 4, 1 pillow of fabric 1, 1 pillow of fabric 4, 1 pillow of fabric 2, 1 pillow of fabric 3, 1 pillow of fabric 1

Row 8: 1 pillow of fabric 1, 2 pillows of fabric 3, 1 pillow of fabric 2, 1 pillow of fabric 4, 1 pillow of fabric 2, 2 pillows of fabric 3, 1 pillow of fabric 1

Row 9: 1 pillow of fabric 1, 3 pillows of fabric 3, 1 pillow of fabric 2, 3 pillows of fabric 3, 1 pillow of fabric 1

Row 10: 1 pillow of fabric 1, 7 pillows of fabric 3, 1 pillow of fabric 1

Row 11: 9 pillows of fabric 1

6 Butting the edges of adjoining pillows together and using a zigzag or overlock stitch, join the pillows together in rows in the correct sequence.

7 Place a small quantity of fibre stuffing in each pillow. Take care, as overstuffing will make it difficult to stitch the pillows together accurately. Pin the openings closed.

8 Butt the edges of adjoining rows together and stitch them together in the same way, closing the open side of each square as you stitch.

Above: The complete Pillow Quilt
Left: Joining the pillows using a Bernina overlocker

PATCHWORK NURSERY QUILT

Kate McEwen made this nursery quilt using four different but harmonising patterns in dress-weight cotton. Here we include two options for this pretty nursery quilt design. This very easy-to-sew quilt is machine-pieced and machine-quilted.

FABRIC SUGGESTIONS

Mix patterns and plain fabrics as well as colours, picking up some of those fabrics in some frilled curtains.

FINISHED SIZE

Quilt: 88 cm x 120 cm
Block size: 14 cm x 14 cm
Total number of blocks: 24

FABRIC QUANTITIES

30 cm of 115 cm wide cream cotton fabric
1.5 m of 115 cm wide cotton fabric for strips, binding and backing
70 cm each of two other 115 cm wide fabrics
88 cm x 120 cm batting

NOTIONS

pencil and ruler
rotary (Olfa) cutter and mat
safety pins, pins and scissors
sewing machine

CUTTING

1 cm seam allowances are included in the cutting instructions

1 Cut 4.4 m of 6 cm wide strips in each of the four fabrics. Join strips to achieve the necessary length.

CONSTRUCTION

2 Join the four strips together lengthways in whatever colour arrangement you like, forming a strip approximately 18 cm wide. Press the seams to one side.

3 Cut the strip into 18 cm lengths, to make twenty-four 18 cm squares.

4 Lay the squares out, in four rows of six, taking care to alternate the direction of the seams in the blocks as shown. Sew the squares into rows, then join the rows to form the quilt top. Press.

5 Measure the width of the quilt, measuring through the centre. Cut two strips of the inner border fabric to this length and 6 cm wide. Sew these to the top and bottom of the quilt top. Measure the length of the quilt top, including the top and bottom borders. Cut two strips of the inner border fabric to this length and 6 cm wide. Sew these to the sides of the quilt.

6 Repeat the process in Step 5 for the outer border, cutting the fabric 10 cm wide.

QUILTING

7 Place the backing fabric face down on a table. Place the batting on top and the quilt top on top of that, facing upwards. Pin-baste the three layers together.

8 Machine-quilt around all the blocks and borders in the seamlines.

FINISHING

9 Measure the width of the quilt as before and cut the binding fabric 6 cm wide to this length. Fold the binding strip over double lengthways, with wrong sides together. Sew the binding to the right side of the top and bottom of the quilt with raw edges even. Repeat for the side bindings.

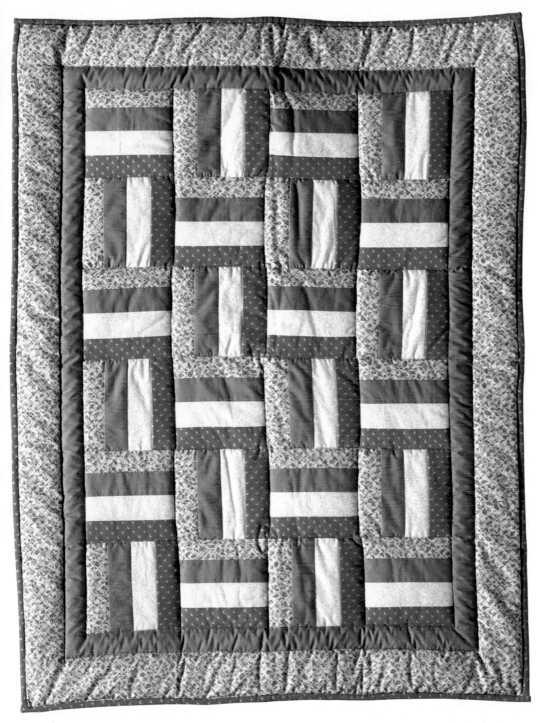

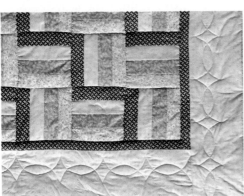

Left: A delightful addition to any nursery
Below left: Try a slightly different arrangement of colours and strips
Below: Keep your baby cosy and warm with a special quilt

CHICKEN WALL QUILT

Strong, clear colours work best for a pictorial quilted wall hanging like this one which uses a mixture of appliqué and piecing. The black borders give the quilt great definition. Designed and made by Doffy White.

FABRIC SUGGESTIONS

Printed and plain cotton fabrics cleverly represent corrugated roofing, feathers and even eggs. The tartan binding adds a whimsical touch.

FINISHED SIZE

Quilt: 1.14 m x 1.18 m

FABRIC QUANTITIES

60 cm x 80 cm ticking for the background
10 cm x 94 cm in four different red prints for the borders
55 cm of 115 cm wide black fabric for the inner borders around the roof
12 cm of 115 cm wide black fabric for the outer borders
four strips tartan fabric 8 cm x 1.20 m for the binding
1.15 m x 1.20 m backing fabric
a variety of scrap fabrics for feathers, eggs, chicken bodies, combs and beaks
120 cm x 125 cm quilter's batting

NOTIONS

13 mm wide black bias binding
sewing thread and quilting thread
pencil, tracing paper and ruler
sewing machine

CUTTING

See the Pull Out Pattern Sheet at the back of the book for the pattern outlines.

1 cm seam allowances are included in the cutting instructions unless stated otherwise.

1 Add 1 cm seam allowances to all the following pieces. Cut out two chicken bodies, using the pattern outline. Cut twenty-five feathers in random sizes and shapes from the red print fabrics. Cut two chicken combs and two chicken beaks from plain fabric, following the pattern outline. Cut nine eggs from plain white fabric.

CONSTRUCTION

2 Cut four strips, each 15 cm wide x 88 cm long from the 85 cm length of black fabric. Place these in pairs and, using a small jar lid, mark the scallops across one long edge of each pair. Round off the space between the scallops. Stitch the strips together along the scalloped edge. Trim the seams and clip into the curves. Turn them to the right side and press the scallops.

3 Cut two more strips from the 85 cm of black fabric, each about 60 cm long by 13 cm wide. Press under 1 cm on one long side of each piece.

4 Open out one folded edge of the bias binding and sew this edge, right sides facing to the right side of all the feathers, bodies, beaks, eggs and combs with the raw edges matching. Note that one comb is reversed. Press the bias binding over to the wrong side, leaving a black border around all the pieces.

5 Lay the ticking background on a table and arrange the scalloped pieces at the top and bottom. Tuck the tops and bottoms of the other two black pieces underneath these scalloped pieces, placing the folded edge towards the centre and angling the lower edge outwards as shown, so that it disappears altogether. This inner appliquéd panel should finish at about 75 cm square. Trim the black panels. Baste them onto the ticking.

6 Position the chicken bodies as shown, tucking under the feathers, combs and beaks. Pin and baste these into place. Pin and baste the eggs into position. Machine-stitch around all the pieces, through all thicknesses.

7 Measure the width of the complete panel through the centre. Cut two 8 cm wide borders plus seam allowances in two different red print fabrics to this length. Stitch them to the top and bottom edges of the trimmed panel. Measure the length of the quilt through the middle and cut two strips, 8 cm wide plus seam allowances, to this length. Stitch them to both sides of the trimmed panel, enclosing the raw ends of the top and bottom borders.

8 Repeat Step 7 for the black borders, joining them to the red ones.

9 Place the backing fabric face down on a table with the batting on top. Place the trimmed panel face up on top. Pin-baste or baste the layers together. Hand-quilt around the borders and all the edges of the appliquéd pieces. Trim off excess batting and backing fabric.

10 Cut two strips of tartan fabric to the length of the quilt and 8 cm wide. Sew the tartan binding down each side edge with right sides together and raw edges even. Turn in 1 cm on remaining long edge of each strip, take the binding over to the wrong side and handsew the folded edge to the previous row of stitching. Repeat for the top and bottom edges of the quilt, folding in the raw ends.

77

QUILTED CUSHIONS

Tonia Todman designed these pieced and quilted cushions as a pair and the only difference between them is in the varying ways the colours and prints have been used. As the lines are all straight, the design is also a pleasing way to show stripes and plaid fabrics. The cushions were made by Martina Oprey.

FABRIC SUGGESTIONS

These cushions effectively combine plain and printed cotton fabrics of the same weight. They were selected from a coordinating range produced especially for patchwork.

FINISHED SIZE

40 cm square, plus piping.

FABRIC QUANTITIES

For each cushion:
20 cm of 115 cm wide fabric for the
    centre square and smaller corner
    squares
46 cm square for back
fabric for bias piping
scrap pieces for side strips

NOTIONS

For each cushion:
cushion insert
1.7 m of piping cord
80 cm fine quilter's batting
30 cm zipper

CUTTING

Do not forget to add 1 cm seam allowances to all the pieces you cut, except for the back panel which has 1 cm seam allowances included.

For each cushion:

1 Cut one 20 cm square for the centre, four 8 cm squares for the corners, four strips 2 cm x 24 cm for the inner strips A, four strips 2 cm x 24 cm for the inner strips B, four strips 6 cm x 24 cm for the outer strips C, two panels 23 cm x 42 cm for the cushion back.

2 Cut sufficient 5 cm wide bias strips to make 1.70 m of bias piping.

CONSTRUCTION

3 Stitch two inner strips A to either side of the centre square, trimming off any excess level with the square.

4 Stitch two remaining strips A to the top and bottom of the centre square, stitching over the ends of the first A strips.

5 Stitch the inner strips B to the outer strips C along one long side. Stitch the B side of one of these pairs to an A strip on one side of the centre square. Stitch another one to the opposite A strip.

6 Stitch an 8 cm square to each end of each remaining joined pair of strips. Centre and stitch each B edge to a remaining A edge, stitching across the ends of the previously sewn-on pairs of strips. Press well.

QUILTING

7 Fold the cushion front diagonally both ways and press a cross into the centre panel of the cushion.

8 Pin-baste the cushion top to the fine batting. Align the edge of the presser foot or your machine's quilting guide with the creases and stitch a triangle in each quarter of the centre panel. Continue making smaller triangles, using the presser foot or the quilting guide as your guide until the space is filled. Using the same technique, stitch squares in the corner squares.

FINISHING

9 Fold the piping strip in half, with wrong sides facing, enclosing the piping cord. Using the zipper foot of your sewing machine, stitch along close to the cord.

10 Baste the piping to the right side of the cushion front, with raw edges matching and the cord 1 cm from the outer edge. Clip cord seam allowance at the corners for ease.

11 Place the two cushion backs together, right sides facing and raw edges matching. Stitch across one 42 cm side taking a 2 cm seam allowance, and leaving a 30 cm gap in the centre for the zipper. Press the seam open. Stitch the zipper into the opening. Open zipper.

12 Place the cushion front and back together, right sides facing. Stitch around the edge of the cushion, following the stitching line for the piping. Clip away excess fabric at corners. Turn the cushion to the right side, place the cushion insert inside and close the zipper.

Below: A quilting guide on your sewing machine is useful for quilting rows
Right: A smart pair of pieced and quilted cushions

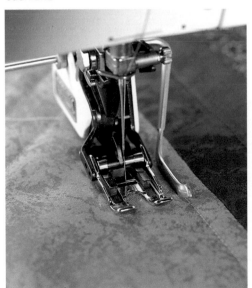

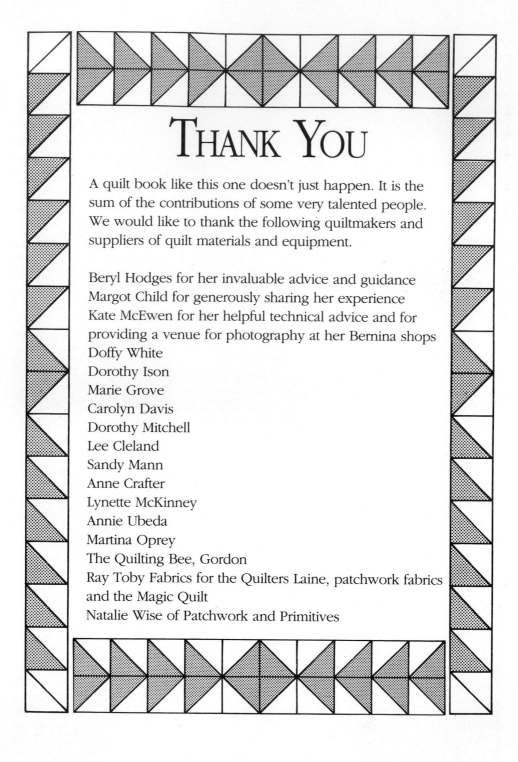

THANK YOU

A quilt book like this one doesn't just happen. It is the sum of the contributions of some very talented people. We would like to thank the following quiltmakers and suppliers of quilt materials and equipment.

Beryl Hodges for her invaluable advice and guidance
Margot Child for generously sharing her experience
Kate McEwen for her helpful technical advice and for providing a venue for photography at her Bernina shops
Doffy White
Dorothy Ison
Marie Grove
Carolyn Davis
Dorothy Mitchell
Lee Cleland
Sandy Mann
Anne Crafter
Lynette McKinney
Annie Ubeda
Martina Oprey
The Quilting Bee, Gordon
Ray Toby Fabrics for the Quilters Laine, patchwork fabrics and the Magic Quilt
Natalie Wise of Patchwork and Primitives